€10--

D1765685

Microsoft®

FrontPage®

2002

10

MINUTE

GUIDE

QUe®

Joe Habraken

Ten Minute Guide to Microsoft® FrontPage® 2002 Copyright © 2002 by Que

International Standard Book Number: 0-7897-2632-7

Library of Congress Catalog Card Number: 2001090287

Printed in the United States of America

First Printing: October 2001

04 03 02 01   4 3 2 1

Trademarks

Warning and Disclaimer

Associate Publisher
Greg Wiegand

Acquisitions Editor
Stephanie J. McComb

Managing Editor
Thomas F. Hayes

Senior Editor
Susan Ross Moore

Copy Editor
Linda Seifert

Indexer
Mandie Frank

Proofreader
Mary Ann Abramson

Technical Editor
Dallas J. Releford

Team Coordinator
Sharry Lee Gregory

Interior Designer
Gary Adair

Cover Designer
Alan Clements

Page Layout
Gloria Schurick

Contents

About the Author

Joe Habraken is a computer technology professional and best-selling author with more than fifteen years of experience in the information technology field as a network administrator, consultant, and educator. His recent publications include *Microsoft Office XP 8-in-1*, *The Absolute Beginner's Guide to Networking (Second Edition)*, and *Practical Cisco Routers*. Joe currently serves as the Director of UNEit, an IT training center for computer industry professionals at the University of New England in Portland, ME.

DEDICATION

To all the fine staff at UNEit; could someone please crank up the air conditioning?

ACKNOWLEDGMENTS

Creating books like this takes a real team effort. I would like to thank Stephanie McComb, our acquisitions editor, who worked very hard to assemble the team that made this book a reality. Also a tip of the hat and a thanks to Dallas Releford, who as the technical editor for the project did a fantastic job making sure that everything was correct and suggested a number of additions that made the book even more technically sound. Finally, a great big thanks to our project editor, Susan Moore, who ran the last leg of the race and made sure the book made it to press on time—what a great team of professionals.

TELL US WHAT YOU THINK!

As the reader of this book, *you* are our most important critic and commentator. We value your opinion and want to know what we're doing right, what we could do better, what areas you'd like to see us publish in, and any other words of wisdom you're willing to pass our way.

As an Associate Publisher for Que, I welcome your comments. You can fax, email, or write me directly to let me know what you did or didn't like about this book—as well as what we can do to make our books stronger.

Please note that I cannot help you with technical problems related to the topic of this book, and that due to the high volume of mail I receive, I might not be able to reply to every message.

When you write, please be sure to include this book's title and author as well as your name and phone or fax number. I will carefully review your comments and share them with the author and editors who worked on the book.

Fax: 317-581-4666

Email: feedback@quepublishing.com

Mail: Associate Publisher
           Que
           201 West 103rd Street
           Indianapolis, IN 46290 USA

Introduction

Microsoft FrontPage 2002 is a powerful Web site design software application that provides an easy-to-use interface and all the tools that you need to build personal and business Web sites. You have the option to create your Web pages from scratch or use wizards that build your Web site with ready-made pages. All you have to do is add the content.

THE WHAT AND WHY OF MICROSOFT FRONTPAGE

Microsoft FrontPage not only provides you with the ability to create your own Web sites, but it also provides features and tools that allow you to easily enhance your Web pages and verify and repair the links that make up your site. You will be able to quickly create exciting Web sites using the following features:

- Web wizards that help you build specialized sites such as corporate Web sites and online discussion sites.

- Special FrontPage components make it easy for you to add banners, navigation bars, and even hit counts to your Web site.

- FrontPage themes allow you to add color, background patterns, and special fonts to the pages in your Web.

- Hyperlink verification can be handled automatically by FrontPage, helping you to make sure that all the links in your Web operate correctly.

- Clip art can be added to your web to provide visual interest. The Clip Art library also includes motion clips and sounds.

While providing you with many complex features, Microsoft FrontPage is easy to learn. It allows you to build powerful Web sites without having to learn HTML. This book will help you understand the possibilities awaiting you with Microsoft FrontPage 2002.

WHY QUE'S *TEN MINUTE GUIDE TO MICROSOFT FRONTPAGE 2002?*

The *Ten Minute Guide to Microsoft FrontPage 2002* can save you precious time while you get to know the different features provided by Microsoft FrontPage. Each lesson is designed to be completed in 10 minutes or less, so you'll be up to snuff on basic and advanced FrontPage features and skills quickly.

Although you can jump around among lessons, starting at the beginning is a good plan. The bare-bones basics are covered first, and more advanced topics are covered later. Following the lessons sequentially will allow you to walk through all the steps of creating and publishing a Web site to the World Wide Web.

INSTALLING FRONTPAGE

You can install Microsoft FrontPage 2002 on a computer running Microsoft Windows 98, Windows NT 4.0., Windows 2000, and Windows XP. Microsoft FrontPage can be purchased as a stand-alone product on its own CD-ROM, or it can be purchased as part of the Microsoft Office XP Special Edition (which comes on several CD-ROMs). Whether you are installing FrontPage as a stand-alone product or as part of the Microsoft Office XP suite, the installation steps are basically the same.

To install FrontPage, follow these steps:

1. Start your computer. Then insert the FrontPage or Microsoft XP Office CD in the CD-ROM drive. The CD-ROM should autostart, providing you with the opening installation screen (for either FrontPage or Office, depending on the CD you are working with).

2. If the CD-ROM does not autostart, choose **Start**, **Run**. in the Run dialog box, type the letter of the CD-ROM drive, followed by **setup** (for example, **d:\setup**). If necessary, use the **Browse** button to locate and select the CD-ROM drive and the setup.exe program.

3. When the Setup Wizard prompts you, enter your name, organization, and CD key in the appropriate box.

4. Choose **Next** to continue.

5. The next wizard screen provides instructions to complete the installation. Complete the installation, select **Next** to advance from screen to screen after providing the appropriate information requested by the wizard.

After you complete the installation from the CD, icons for FrontPage and any other Office applications you may have installed will be provided on the Windows Start menu. Lesson 2, "Getting Familiar with FrontPage," provides you with a step-by-step guide to starting FrontPage 2002.

Conventions Used in This Book

To help you move through the lessons easily, these conventions are used:

On-screen text	On-screen text appears in bold type.
Text you should type	Information you need to type appears in a different, bold typeface.
Items you select	Commands, options, and icons you are to select and keys you are to press appear in bold type.

In telling you to choose menu commands, this book uses the format *menu title, menu command.* For example, the statement "choose **File**, **Properties**" means "open the File menu and select the Properties command."

In addition to those conventions the *Ten Minute Guide to Microsoft FrontPage 2002* uses the following icons to identify helpful information:

PLAIN ENGLISH PLEASE

New or unfamiliar terms are defined in term sidebars.

TIP

Read these tips for ideas that cut corners and confusion.

CAUTION

This icon identifies areas where new users often run into trouble; these tips offer practical solutions to those problems.

LESSON 1

What's New in FrontPage 2002

In this lesson, you are introduced to FrontPage's powerful Web site and Web page design features, and you learn what's new in FrontPage 2002.

GETTING THE MOST OUT OF FRONTPAGE 2002

Microsoft FrontPage is a full-featured Web design application that provides you with all the tools you need to create your own Web page or Web site and get it onto the Web. Wizards and templates are provided that make it easy for you to create simple, personal Web sites or complex Web sites for your business. FrontPage not only makes it easy for you to create your own Web pages and sites, it also enables you to test and troubleshoot the site before publishing it to the World Wide Web.

Web pages and sites must be created in the HTML (Hypertext Markup Language) programming language for them to function when viewed in a Web browser such as Microsoft Internet Explorer. FrontPage helps you create sophisticated Web pages and sites without having to learn HTML.

PLAIN ENGLISH

> **Web Page**   A single page containing text and graphics that has been labeled with the appropriate HTML coding for the Web.

PLAIN ENGLISH

> **Web Site**   A collection of linked Web pages containing various content that can easily be navigated using a Web browser.

FrontPage provides a number of features that make it easy for you to design your Web site and Web pages without creating each page and page feature using HTML. Some of the FrontPage features that you will explore in this book are

- Wizards: Wizards can help you quickly build the basic structure of your Web site. Wizards such as the Corporate Presence Wizard and the Discussion Web Wizard walk you through the process of creating specialized Web sites and the pages that they contain. You will work with the FrontPage wizards in Lesson 3, "Creating a New Web Site."

PLAIN ENGLISH

> **Wizard**   A feature that guides you step by step through a particular process in FrontPage, such as creating a new Web site.

- Themes: Themes provide the "look" for your entire Web site or individual pages in a Web site. A FrontPage theme provides a color scheme for a Web page, graphics, and background patterns. Themes will be discussed in Lesson 11, "Using FrontPage Themes."

PLAIN ENGLISH

> **Theme**   A collection of color and design attributes that are identified by a theme name. A particular theme can be applied to an entire Web site or to individual pages on a Web site.

- Frames: Frames are used to divide the area shown in a Web browser into separate elements called frames. Each frame can show different information or even a separate page of information. Each frame can have its own scroll bars and other elements. Frames are discussed Lesson 15, "Using Frames on Web Pages."

Whether you are a new FrontPage user or are familiar with previous versions of FrontPage, you will also find that FrontPage 2002 provides all the tools you need to manipulate text, images, and other Web page elements. Many of the features related to text and images are similar to those provided by other Microsoft products such as Microsoft Word, making FrontPage a familiar environment even for the new Web page designer.

NEW FEATURES IN FRONTPAGE 2002

FrontPage 2002 also builds on the features found in the previous versions of FrontPage by offering a number of new features that make it easier for you to quickly design Web sites and Web pages. New features in FrontPage 2002 range from the task pane (which makes it easier for you to copy and paste information and insert images onto your Web pages) to voice dictation and commands and to new ways to quickly get help.

Let's take a look at task panes and the new voice feature provided by FrontPage. You will have the opportunity to explore the new FrontPage help system in Lesson 10, "Getting Help in Microsoft FrontPage."

INTRODUCING TASK PANES

One of the biggest changes to the FrontPage environment (and all the Microsoft Office XP member applications such as Word 2002, Excel 2002, and PowerPoint 2002) is the introduction of the Office task pane. The task pane is a special pane that appears on the right side of the FrontPage application window when you access certain features. For example, when you insert clip art onto a Web page, you will use the Clip Art task pane. It is used to provide access to a number of FrontPage features that were formerly controlled using dialog boxes.

For example, when you work with clip art in FrontPage, you will access the various clip art files using the Clip Art task pane, which is shown in Figure 1.1.

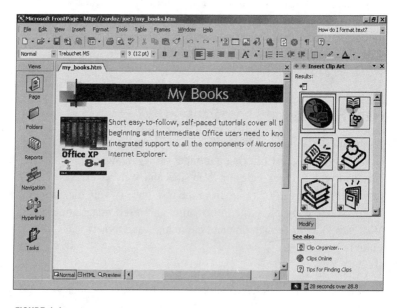

FIGURE 1.1
The Clip Art task pane is used to place clip art onto your Web pages.

Another task pane that you will run across as you use FrontPage is the Office Clipboard. The Office Clipboard allows you to copy or cut multiple items from a Web page then paste them into a new location in the current Web page or a new Web page. Specific task panes will be discussed in the appropriate lessons in this book.

INTRODUCING VOICE DICTATION AND VOICE COMMANDS

One of the most exciting new features in FrontPage 2002 (and the entire Office XP suite) is voice dictation and voice-activated commands. If your computer is outfitted with a sound card, speakers, and a microphone (or a microphone with an earphone headset), you can dictate information into your FrontPage documents. You also can use voice commands to activate the menu system.

Before you can really take advantage of the Speech feature, you must provide it with some training so that it can more easily recognize your speech patterns and intonation. After the Speech feature is trained, you can effectively use it to dictate text entries or access various application commands without a keyboard or mouse.

CAUTION

> **Requirements for Getting the Most Out of the Speech Feature**   To make the Speech feature useful, you will need a fairly high-quality microphone. Microsoft suggests a microphone/headset combination. The Speech feature also requires a powerful computer. Microsoft suggests using a computer with 128MB of RAM and a Pentium II (or later) processor running at a minimum of 400MHz. A computer that meets or exceeds these standards should be capable of getting the most out of the Speech feature.

If you are new to FrontPage, you may want to explore the other lessons in this book before you attempt to use the Speech feature. Having a good understanding of how FrontPage operates and the features that it provides will allow you to then get the most out of the Speech feature.

TRAINING THE SPEECH FEATURE

The first time you start the Speech feature in FrontPage, you are required to configure and train the feature. Follow these steps to get the Speech feature up and running:

1. In FrontPage, select the **Tools** menu and select **Speech**. The Welcome to Office Speech Recognition dialog box appears. To begin the process of setting up your microphone and training the Speech feature, click the **Next** button.

2. The first screen of the Microphone Wizard appears. It asks you to be sure that your microphone and speakers are connected to your computer. If you have a headset microphone, this screen shows you how to adjust the microphone for use. Click **Next** to continue.

3. The next wizard screen asks you to read a short text passage so that your microphone volume level can be adjusted (see Figure 1.2). When you have finished reading the text, click **Next** to continue.

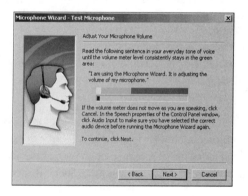

FIGURE 1.2
The Microphone Wizard adjusts the volume of your microphone.

4. On the next screen, you are told that if you have a headset microphone, you can click **Finish** and proceed to the speech recognition training. If you have a different type of microphone, you are asked to read another text passage. The text is then played back to you. This is to determine whether the microphone is placed at an appropriate distance from your mouth; when you get a satisfactory playback, click **Finish**.

When you finish working with the Microphone Wizard, the Voice Training Wizard appears. This wizard collects samples of your speech and, in essence, educates the Speech feature as to how you speak.

To complete the voice training process, follow these steps:

1. After reading the information on the opening screen, click **Next** to begin the voice training process.

2. On the next screen, you are asked to provide your gender and age (see Figure 1.3). After specifying the correct information, click **Next**.

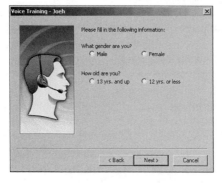

FIGURE 1.3
Supply the voice trainer with your gender and age.

3. On the next wizard screen, you are provided an overview of how the voice training will proceed. You are also provided with directions on how to pause the training session. Click **Next**.

4. The next wizard screen reminds you to adjust your micro-
    phone. You are also reminded that you need a quiet room
    when training the Speech feature. When you are ready to
    begin training the speech recognition feature, click **Next**.

5. On the next screen, you are asked to read some text. As the
    wizard recognizes each word, the word is highlighted. After
    finishing with this screen, continue by clicking **Next**.

6. You are asked to read text on several subsequent screens.
    Words are selected as the wizard recognizes them.

7. When you complete the training screens, your profile is
    updated. Click **Finish** on the wizard's final screen.

You are now ready to use the Speech feature. The next two sections
discuss using the Voice Dictation and Voice Command features.

CAUTION

The Speech Feature Works Better Over Time   Be advised
that the voice feature's performance improves as you use
it. As you learn to pronounce your words more carefully,
the Speech feature tunes itself to your speech patterns.
You might need to do additional training sessions to
fine-tune the Speech feature.

USING VOICE DICTATION

When you are ready to start dictating text into a Web page, put on
your headset microphone or place your standalone microphone in the
proper position that you determined when you used the Microphone
Wizard. When you're ready to go, select the **Tools** menu and then
select **Speech**. The Language bar appears (see Figure 1.4); click the
Dictation button on the toolbar (if the Dictation button is not already
activated or depressed).

After you enable the Dictation button, you can begin dictating your
text into the FrontPage document. Figure 1.4 shows text being dictated

into a Web page. When you want to put a line break into the text, say "new line." Punctuation is placed in the document by saying the name of a particular punctuation mark, such as "period" or "comma."

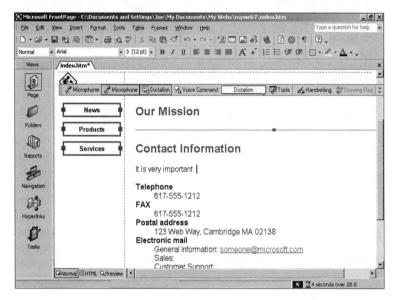

FIGURE 1.4
Dictating text into FrontPage.

CAUTION

How Do I Insert the Word "Comma" Rather Than the Punctuation Mark?   Because certain keywords, such as "period" or "comma," are used to insert punctuation during dictation, you must spell these words out if you want to include them in the text. To do this, say "spelling mode," and then spell out the word, such as c-o-m-m-a. As soon as you dictate an entire word, the spelling mode is ended.

When you have finished dictating into the document, click the **Micro-phone** button on the Language bar (the second Microphone button from the left; the first is used to select the current speech driver, which you can leave as the default). When you click the **Microphone** button, the Language bar collapses, hiding the **Dictation** and the **Voice Command** buttons. You can also stop Dictation mode by saying "microphone."

You can minimize the Language bar by clicking the **Minimize** button on the right end of the bar. This sends the Language bar to the Windows System Tray (it appears as a small square icon marked EN, if you are using the English version of FrontPage).

With the Language bar minimized in the System Tray, you can quickly open it when you need it. Click the **Language Bar** icon in the System Tray, and then select **Show the Language Bar** (which is the only choice provided when you click on the Language Bar icon).

USING VOICE COMMANDS

Another tool the Speech feature provides is voice command. You can open and select menus in an application and even navigate dialog boxes using voice commands.

To use voice commands, open the Language bar (click **Tools**, **Speech**). Click the **Microphone** icon, if necessary, to expand the Language bar. Then, click the **Voice Command** icon on the bar (or say "voice command").

To open a particular menu such as the Format menu, say "format." Then, to open a particular submenu such as Font, say "font." In the case of these voice commands, the Font dialog box opens.

You can then navigate a particular dialog box using voice commands. In the Font dialog box, for example, to change the size of the font, say "size"; this activates the Size box that controls font size. Then, say the size of the font, such as "14." You can also activate other font attrib-utes in the dialog box in this manner. Say the name of the area of the dialog box you want to use, and then say the name of the feature you want to turn on or select.

When you have finished working with a particular dialog box, say "OK," (or "Cancel" or "Apply," as needed) and the dialog box closes and provides you with the features you selected in the dialog box. When you have finished using voice commands, say "microphone," or click the **Microphone** icon on the Language bar.

Believe it or not, you can also activate buttons on the various toolbars using voice commands. For example, you could turn on bold by saying, "bold." The Bold button on the Formatting toolbar becomes active. To turn bold off, say, "bold" again.

In this lesson, you were introduced to FrontPage 2002 and some of the new features available in this latest version of FrontPage, such as task panes and the Speech feature. In the next lesson, you learn how to start FrontPage and you become familiar with the FrontPage workspace.

LESSON 2
Getting Familiar with FrontPage

In this lesson, you learn how to start Microsoft FrontPage and navigate the FrontPage window. You also learn about some of the special tools that FrontPage provides for designing Web sites.

STARTING FRONTPAGE

When you first start Microsoft FrontPage, you will be asked to create a new Web site. Once this Web site has been designated, you are free to create the various pages that will be contained in the site. The first step in the Web creation process is starting FrontPage; follow these steps:

1. From the Windows desktop, click **Start** and select **Programs**. The Programs menu appears.

2. To start FrontPage, click the **FrontPage** icon. The FrontPage application window opens.

UNDERSTANDING THE FRONTPAGE ENVIRONMENT

When you start FrontPage, the FrontPage application window opens (see Figure 2.1). The overall geography of the FrontPage window is similar to that of other Microsoft Office applications, such as Excel and Word. In fact, you will find that when you create and edit Web pages and Web sites in the FrontPage window, you use many of the techniques and tools you use in a word processing application such as Microsoft Word.

Toolbars   Title bar   Menu bar

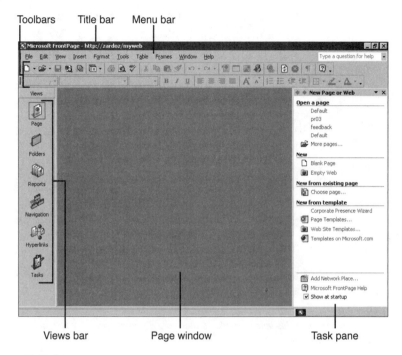

Views bar   Page window   Task pane

FIGURE 2.1
The FrontPage window is where you create your Web pages and Web sites.

FrontPage does have an area of its window that is distinct from other
Office applications. The Views bar on the left side of the FrontPage
window enables you to quickly switch between different views associated with the currently open Web site. For example, the Page view
enables you to view and edit the current Web page (see Figure 2.2).
Another view, the Navigation view, enables you to view all the pages
in the current Web site and see how they are linked to form a complete
site (for more about the views available on the Views bar, see
Lesson 2, "Creating a New Web Site").

FIGURE 2.2
*The Views pane enables you to quickly switch to a different view of a Web site,
such as the Page view.*

CAUTION

Don't Confuse the Views Bar with the View Tabs
FrontPage uses the term *view* in two contexts. The Views
bar enables you to change your view of your Web site by
changing the entire View pane to a Page view, a
Navigation view, and so on. Within Page view, the View
tabs enable you to change the view for the current Web
page to a regular view, an HTML code view, and a preview (for more about the View tabs, see Lesson 4,
"Working with Web Pages").

You might notice that the largest area of the window is currently
blank; a new, blank Web page (serving the same function as a blank
document window in Word) appears in the FrontPage window when
you start the application. You can use this blank page to build a new

Web page from scratch, or you can use one of the templates that FrontPage offers (for more about creating individual Web pages and the use of templates, see Lesson 4).

Table 2.1 describes the elements you see in the FrontPage application window.

TABLE 2.1   Elements of the FrontPage Window

Element	Description
Title bar	Includes the name of the application (FrontPage) and the Minimize, Maximize, and Close buttons.
Task pane	The task pane is used for many FrontPage features, such as creating a new Web page and adding graphics to a Web. Lesson 3 provides an introduction to the task pane.
Menu bar	Contains menus of commands you can use to perform tasks in the program.
Toolbar	Includes icons that serve as shortcuts for common commands, such as Save, Print, and Spelling.
Page window	This is where you create and edit the current Web page.
Scrollbars	The horizontal scrollbar is used to scroll your view of the current page from left to right or vice versa. The vertical scroll-bar is used to scroll up and down through the current page.
Views bar	Provides quick access to the different views associated with the current Web site. The Views bar is discussed in detail in Lesson 3.

USING COMMANDS AND FEATURES IN FRONTPAGE

As with the other applications in Microsoft Office, FrontPage provides several ways to access the commands and features used to create your Web pages. You can access these commands using the menus on the menu bar and the buttons on the various toolbars that FrontPage supplies.

You can also access many FrontPage commands using shortcut menus. These menus are accessed by right-clicking a particular page element. The shortcut menu appears with a list of commands related to the item that you are currently working on, such as text or a picture.

EXITING FRONTPAGE

When you work in FrontPage, you will find that a Web site consists of multiple, linked Web pages (although a simple Web site can consist of one Web page). The lessons that follow in this section of the book walk you through the creation of a simple Web site from beginning to Web publication.

When you have finished your initial survey of the FrontPage application window, or whenever you have finished your work in the program, you will want to exit the software. You can exit FrontPage by selecting **File**, **Exit**, or you can close FrontPage with one click of the mouse by clicking the FrontPage **Close** (x) button in the upper-right corner of the application window.

When you close FrontPage, you are prompted to save any work that you have done in the application window. If you were just experimenting as you read through this lesson, you can click **No**. The current Web page is not saved, and the FrontPage application window closes. All the ins and outs of actually saving your Web pages and the structure of your Web site are covered in Lesson 3.

In this lesson, you learned how to start FrontPage and explored the various parts of the FrontPage window. You also learned how to exit the FrontPage program. In the next lesson, you learn how to create a new Web site.

LESSON 3
Creating a New Web Site

In this lesson, you learn how to create a new Web site using the FrontPage Web Wizards. You also become familiar with the different Web views provided on the FrontPage Views bar.

USING THE WEB SITE WIZARDS

FrontPage provides several wizards you can use to create your own Web site (in FrontPage, a Web site is called a *web*). These wizards can create different kinds of sites, ranging from the personal to the professional, or they can help you add certain types of functions to your current Web site (such as a discussion page or a page for project management).

Table 3.1 lists the Web Wizards that are available and the type of web they help you create.

Table 3.1 Selecting a Web Wizard for Your New Web Site

Web Wizard	Site Created
One Page Web	A web consisting of a single blank page (the home page).
Corporate Presence	A multipage web with pages for products and services and links for e-mail messages to the company.
Customer Support	A web that provides a FAQ (frequently asked questions) page, a suggestion page, a download page, and a search page to help support customers using the site.

Table 3.1   (continued)

Web Wizard	Site Created
Discussion Web	A web consisting of a discussion page that allows visitors to your site to post and read discussion messages.
Database Interface	A web that connects to a database and allows you to view and update records.
Empty Web	A web consisting of no pages.
Import Web	A web based on imported files from a Web site created in another program or directly from the World Wide Web.
Personal Web	A multipage web consisting of interests, photos, and links pages.
Project Web	A multipage web used to manage a particular project. A schedule page, a discussion page, and other project management pages are created. This type of site would typically be used on an intranet (a corporation's private web).

When you work with the various wizards, you will find that they provide you with blank pages, partially completed pages, or pages containing text, links, and picture placeholders. In all cases, you must add and edit material in the site to complete your web before you can publish it to the World Wide Web where Web users can access it.

Remember that when you provide a name for the web you are going to create using the wizard, you are actually creating a folder on your computer where the web will reside. Webs do not consist of a single file like an Excel worksheet or Word document does. Webs consist of several page files, picture files, and other elements. When you specify the name for the web, you are making a place for FrontPage to store all the files that make your web look the way it does. A complex web can contain many files, so be sure you have plenty of space on the drive that you use to store the web.

CREATING A NEW WEB

The various Web Wizards that you can use to walk you through web creation determine the level of sophistication of your new web. Although the wizards act in similar ways, the more complex the site, the more questions you have to answer and the more steps you have to complete before the site is created. For example, the Personal Web Wizard provides a fast and easy avenue to a simple Web site for your own use, whereas the Corporate Web Wizard helps you create a complex web that contains a great deal of information (that you provide) about the company that the site is for.

CAUTION

> **Close the Open Blank Page Before Creating a New Web**
> When you start FrontPage, it automatically opens a new blank web page for you and displays it in the Page view (discussed later in this lesson). When you create your new web using a wizard, this page does not become part of the actual web, but it still takes the theme and attributes of the web you create. You might want to close this blank page (click the **Close** button in the upper-right corner of the page) before you build your site. This can prevent confusion caused by a page that appears in the Page view but is not really part of the web you have created.

To create a site using one of the wizards, follow these steps:

1. With the FrontPage application running on the Windows desktop, select the **File** menu and point at **New**. This opens the New page or Web task pane. Select Web Site Templates from the **New from Templates** section. The Web Site Templates dialog box opens showing the Web Site Wizards (see Figure 3.1).

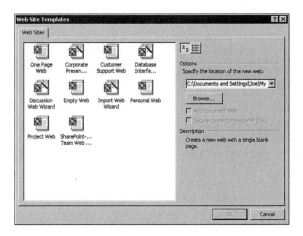

FIGURE 3.1
The Web Site Templates dialog box is where you select the wizard you want to use to build your new web.

2. Select one of the wizard icons in the dialog box, such as **Corporate Presence Wizard**.

3. In the **Specify the Location of the New Web** text box in the **Options** section, specify a name and location for the new web. The default main folder for FrontPage webs is My Webs; however, you can use the **Browse** button to select a new location.

4. Click **OK** to begin the web creation process.

5. Depending on the wizard you selected, your next action begins either with editing and enhancing the Web pages that the wizard creates or answering some questions that the wizard poses before it creates the pages. For example, in the case of the Corporate Presence Web (and other business-related webs such as the Customer Support site), a wizard screen appears, describing the purpose of the wizard. Click **Next** to continue.

6. Answer the questions on each wizard screen and click **Next**
   to continue. Figure 3.2 shows a screen from the Corporate
   Presence Web Wizard in which it asks you to determine the
   topic areas that should appear on the new web's home page.

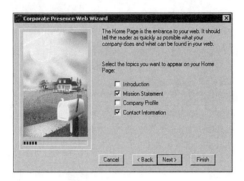

FIGURE 3.2
*The wizard screens let you determine the pages in the web as well as topic areas
and items found on individual pages.*

7. Depending on the wizard that you chose to create your new
   web, you might be asked to select a theme for your new site.
   FrontPage themes provide design elements and color
   schemes that can really help you create eye-catching webs.
   Themes are discussed in Lesson 11, "Using FrontPage
   Themes." After you have completed all the wizard's ques-
   tions, the final wizard screen provides a Finish button. Click
   Finish to end the web creation process.

UNDERSTANDING THE WEB VIEWS

When you complete your new web, you are taken to the Navigation
view of the web, which shows all the pages that were created for your
new site and their relationship to other pages in the site. The site consists of a home page and several other pages that branch from the
home page (and are subordinate to it). Figure 3.3 shows the

Navigation view of a web created using the Personal Web Wizard. Each wizard creates a different number of pages for the site and arranges them in a manner that depends on the purpose of the web.

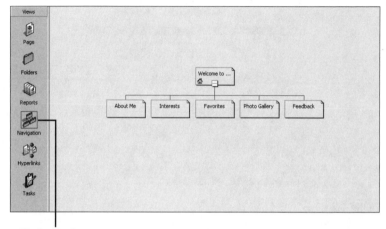

Navigation icon
on the Views bar

FIGURE 3.3
The various wizards end the creation process by showing your new web pages and their configuration in the Navigation view.

CAUTION

Some Wizards Dump You into the Task View   The Corporate Presence Wizard provides an option on the second-to-last wizard screen to take you to the Task view rather than to the Navigation view. If you do not deselect the check box for Task view, you will end up there on completion of the web. The different views available to you in FrontPage are covered in the remainder of this lesson.

The key to completing a web that has been created using a web wizard is understanding how the various views on the FrontPage Views bar are used as you edit and enhance the new web. Each view provides a different information set that shows you how the overall construction of the web is progressing. These views are defined in the sections that follow. You also use these views in the subsequent lessons that discuss FrontPage.

THE NAVIGATION VIEW

The Navigation view (refer to Figure 3.3) enables you to see all the pages in the web in a flowchart format, which gives you the hierarchy for the site. (This view is usually the default view for a site created using one of the wizards.) The home page for the site is at the top of the hierarchy, and all pages that branch from the home page are shown below the home page with a connecting line. FrontPage calls the pages that are below the home page in the web *child pages*.

Child pages are not limited to the home page, however, and any page in the Web site can have child pages. A page that has child pages is called a *parent page*.

You can drag and drop pages in the Navigation view to change their location in the web structure. New pages created for a site are inserted into the web in this manner (see Lesson 11 for more about inserting new pages into a Web site in the Navigation view).

To move to the Navigation view from any other FrontPage view, click the **Navigation** icon on the Views bar.

THE PAGE VIEW

The Page view is used to view and edit a particular page in your web. You use the Page view when you add text, pictures, or other objects to the individual Web pages in the site. The Page view is similar to an Excel worksheet window or a Word document window. It provides a workspace.

To enter the Page view for a specific page in the Web, follow these steps:

1. Go to the Navigation view by clicking the **Navigation** icon on the Views bar (refer to Figure 3.3).

2. Double-click a particular page in the Navigation view. The page opens in the Page view (as shown in Figure 3.4). The look of the page depends on the theme that you chose.

FIGURE 3.4
The Page view is where you focus on a particular page in the web and edit and enhance it.

When you are in the Page view, you can edit the current page as needed (see details in Lesson 4).

TIP

> **Quickly Return to the Previously Opened Page**   If you open a particular page in the Page view by double-clicking it in the Navigation view (or Folders view) and then move to a different view (such as returning to the Navigation view), you can quickly return to the previously opened page by clicking the **Page View** icon on the Views bar.

THE FOLDERS VIEW

The Folders view shows the folders and files in the current web. When you create a web using one of the wizards, several folders and files are created (the files created depend on the wizard that you used).

Click the **Folders** icon in the Views bar to view the folders and files in the web. Figure 3.5 shows the folders and files that are created when you use the Personal Web Wizard to create a new web.

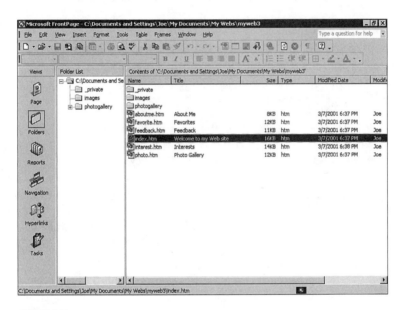

FIGURE 3.5
The Folders view enables you to view the folders and files contained in the current web.

The folders created for any of your new webs (no matter which wizard you use) consist of the following:

- **Web Folder**—This is designated by the name that you provided for the web's location in the Specify the Location of the New Web box in the New dialog box.

- **Private Folder**—This folder is created to hold any data that is input into special forms or other data input objects that you place on a page or pages in your Web site. Because the folder is private, a visitor to your Web site cannot gain access to the information that it holds.

- **Images Folder**—This folder provides a place to save pictures and clip art that are part of the Web site. Any images placed in the web by the wizard are contained in this folder.

Files that are contained in the web can also be seen in the Folders view. Each web typically contains an index.htm file that serves as the home page for the web; the other pages in the web depend on the wizard that was used (each with the .htm extension, which means the page is an HTML document).

You can delete files from the web in the Folders view (select the file and press **Delete**). You can also open pages in the Folders view by double-clicking them. They open in the Page view.

THE REPORTS VIEW

The Reports view enables you to view statistics and other information related to your web. These statistical reports are created automatically when you create the web, and they are updated as you work on the web. To view the statistics for your site, click the **Reports View** icon on the Views bar.

Figure 3.6 shows the Reports view for a personal web. Statistics such as the number of files and pictures in the web are reported as *mini-reports*. Other data provided include unverified links in the web (these usually consist of links to other Web sites on the World Wide Web that have not yet been verified by going online with your web).

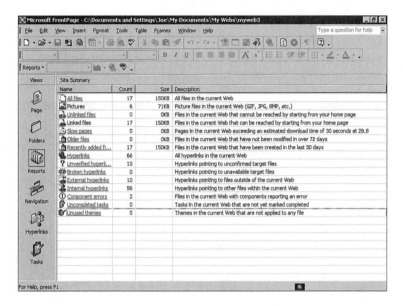

FIGURE 3.6
The Reports view provides you with important statistics related to your web.

The Reporting toolbar enables you to change the statistics displayed in the Reports window (it appears directly below the other FrontPage toolbars). The default list for the Reports view is the Site Summary (refer to Figure 3.6), which shows all the statistics. If you want to view a certain statistic, such as unlinked files (in the web), click the drop-down box on the Reports toolbar and select the statistic—in this example, **Unlinked Files**—from the **Problems** list. These files are listed. Any views found in the Site Summary view can be viewed alone by selecting the appropriate report title from the toolbar drop-down list.

THE HYPERLINKS VIEW

The Hyperlinks view enables you to view the hyperlinks from a particular page in the site to other pages in the site and to other Web sites on the World Wide Web. Figure 3.7 shows the Hyperlinks view for the

Favorites page in a Personal Web site. The page has internal links to the other pages in the web (so that you can quickly go to those pages). It also contains external links that enable you to jump to other sites found on the World Wide Web.

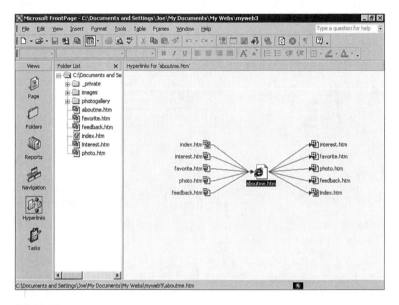

FIGURE 3.7
The Hyperlinks view shows you the internal and external hyperlinks on a specific page in your web.

To go to the Hyperlinks view for a page in your web, be sure that you first select the page in the Folders view or the Navigation view. Then click the **Hyperlinks View** icon on the Views bar. The page and its hyperlinks are displayed. Creating and managing hyperlinks is discussed in Lesson 9, "Working with Hyperlinks."

The Tasks View

The Tasks view enables you to see tasks that are used to help you complete various aspects of your Web site. You can create tasks related to specific pages in the web or items on a Web page, such as a picture or other item. When you start a task that appears on your Tasks list, the task automatically opens the page or goes to the item on the page for which the task was created. Some of the wizards, such as the Corporate Presence Wizard, automatically create a list of tasks that is used to make sure all aspects of the new web are addressed before the web is placed on the World Wide Web for viewing. Tasks are covered in more detail in Lesson 18, "Completing and Publishing Your Web Site."

To go to the Tasks view, click the **Tasks View** icon on the Views bar. Figure 3.8 shows the tasks that were created when the Corporate Presence Wizard was used to create a new web.

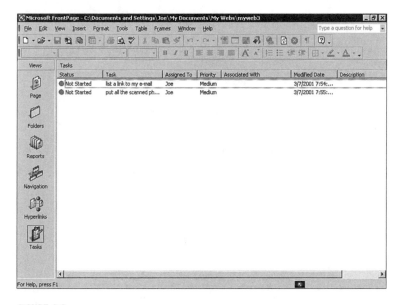

FIGURE 3.8
The Tasks view enables you to create and monitor tasks that are related to the completion of your web.

You might find that you use different views provided by the Views bar as you create or fine-tune your webs. These views are visited and revisited in the other lessons found in this book.

In this lesson, you learned how to create a web using the FrontPage web wizards. You also learned how to navigate the views provided on the FrontPage Views bar and how each view gives you different information about your Web site. In the next lesson, you learn how to create new pages for your web and insert them into the Web site hierarchy.

LESSON 4
Working with Web Pages

In this lesson, you learn how to create new Web pages using the FrontPage templates and how to delete pages and import pages created in other applications.

CREATING A NEW WEB PAGE

FrontPage makes it easy for you to create new Web pages and place them into your web. You can create blank pages or pages that use a FrontPage template. These templates provide you with pages that can add functionality to your Web site.

To create a new page in a web, follow these steps:

1. To open the web where you want to place the new page, select the **File** menu and point at **Recent Webs**; from the cascading menu that appears, select the web you want to open.

> **CAUTION**
>
> **My Web Isn't on the Recent Webs Menu!**   If you have created more than four webs using FrontPage, there is a good chance your most infrequently used webs will no longer appear on the Recent Webs menu, which shows only the last four webs. To open webs not listed, select **File, Open Web**. Use the Open Web dialog box to specify the location for the web. When you have located the web, select it and then click **Open**.

2. With the appropriate web open, you can now create a new page for the web. First, click the **Page View** icon in the View bar to go to the Page view.

3. Select the **File** menu, point at **New**, and the New Page or Web task pane opens. Under **New from Template**, select **Page Templates**, which opens the Page Templates dialog box (see Figure 4.1).

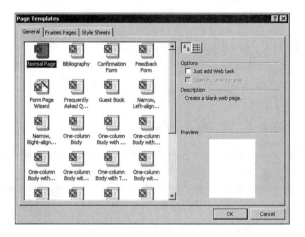

FIGURE 4.1
The General tab of the Page Templates dialog box is where you select the template for your new page.

4. The new page templates are available on the General tab of the Page Templates dialog box. Click the template that you want to use for your new page. Then click **OK** to create the new page.

The new page appears in the FrontPage Page view. Figure 4.2 shows a two-column page that was created using the Two-Column Body template. The templates create pages that contain placeholder text and other items that you can modify. (Working with text on your pages is covered in Lesson 5, "Working with Text in FrontPage.")

FIGURE 4.2
The new page appears in the FrontPage editing window in the Page view.

You will also find that the new page (even though it's not included in
the navigational structure of your web yet) embraces the theme that
you assigned to the current web. (FrontPage themes are covered later
in this lesson.)

Now that you have the new page, you need to save it. Follow these
steps:

1. Click the **Save** button on the FrontPage toolbar. The Save As
   dialog box opens.

2. Type a filename for your new page into the **File Name** box.

3. You also should change the page title for the new page. This
   title appears in the Web browser when you view the particular page on the World Wide Web. To change the page title,
   click the **Change** button. The Set Page Title dialog box opens
   (see Figure 4.3).

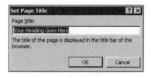

FIGURE 4.3
Type the page title that you want to appear in the Web browser when the page is viewed on the World Wide Web.

4. Type the new page title and click **OK**. You are returned to the Save As dialog box. Click **Save** to complete the process.

Inserting a New Page into the Web

After you've created and saved the new page, you must make the page part of the current web. You might think creating the page when the current web is open in FrontPage should have taken care of that, but it doesn't.

You add the page to the current web by linking the page to either your site's home page (which in most cases will have the name index.htm) or to any other subordinate page in the web.

To add the new page to the navigational structure of your web, follow these steps:

1. Click the **Navigation** icon on the Views bar. The current navigational structure of your page appears.

2. To the left of the Navigation view, a Folder List should appear. If you don't see a list of all the pages available in the web (in the Folder List), click the **Folder List** button on the toolbar.

3. To add the new page to the structure of the web, locate the file in the Folder List, and then drag the file onto the Navigation view, placing the box that represents the file underneath your home page. Figure 4.4 shows a page named "all about whales.htm" being added to the web structure.

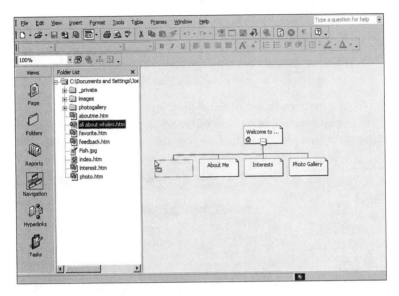

FIGURE 4.4
The Navigation view makes it easy for you to add new pages to your web.

After the page has been added to the web structure, it appears as a page box, as the other pages in the web appear when you are using the Navigation view. If you want to view the page itself, double-click its page box in the Navigation view and it will open in Page view.

DELETING A PAGE FROM THE WEB

Deleting a page from the web is best done in the Navigation view. This not only allows you to quickly delete the page from the navigational structure of the web, but it also removes the appropriate HTML document from the Folder List at the same time.

To delete a page from your web, follow these steps:

1. Click the **Navigation** icon on the Views bar to go to the Navigation view.

2. Click the page that you want to remove from the web (in the Navigation window).

3. Press the **Delete** key on the keyboard. The Delete Page dialog box appears.

4. You have the choice of removing the page from the navigational structure of the web (this does not delete the page file) or deleting the page from the web (this removes it from the structure and deletes the file). Select the appropriate option button in the Delete Page dialog box, as shown in Figure 4.5.

FIGURE 4.5
You can easily remove a page from the web in the Navigation view.

5. Click **OK**. The page is removed from the structure. (The file is deleted if Delete This Page from the Web was selected in the dialog box.)

IMPORTING FILES FROM OTHER APPLICATIONS

You can also import page files into your web that you create in other applications. For example, suppose you designed a Web page in Microsoft Word and saved the document as an HTML file. You can easily import that particular file into the current web.

To import a file into the current web, follow these steps:

1. Select the **File** menu and select **Import**. The Import dialog box appears.

2. Click the **Add File** button. The Add File to Import List dialog box appears.

3. Use the **Look In** drop-down box to locate the drive that holds the file you want to import, and then navigate the folders in the main window until you reach the file's exact location. After selecting the file, click the **OK** button.

4. The filename appears in the Import dialog box (see Figure 4.6). Repeat steps 2 and 3 if you want to add more files to the Import list.

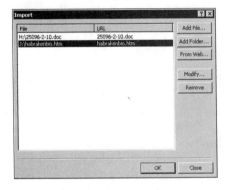

FIGURE 4.6
You can import one or several files into the current web.

5. When you have added all the files to the Import list that you want to import into the current web, click the **OK** button.

The file (or files) is imported into the current web. You can find the files listed in the Folder List of your web. The files then must be made part of the web's navigational structure. Go to the Navigation view and drag the file or files from the Folder List and add them to the Navigation window as discussed earlier in this lesson.

In this lesson, you learned how to create new pages for your web; you also learned to delete unwanted pages from your web and import files from other applications. In the next lesson, you learn how to work with text in FrontPage.

LESSON 5
Working with Text in FrontPage

In this lesson, you learn how to add, edit, and format text on your Web pages, including the creation of your own styles. You also learn how to change the page names for pages in your web.

INSERTING AND MODIFYING TEXT

Working with text in FrontPage is similar to working with text in any word processor, particularly Microsoft Word. Many of the text commands and features that you find in Word are also available in FrontPage (or any of the other Microsoft Office suite products such as Excel or PowerPoint).

If you create your Web pages using a wizard, or if you create a new page using a template, you will see placeholder text on the pages or page. A great deal of the text work you do in FrontPage is replacing placeholder text with your own text. When you replace placeholder text with your own text, the formatting (font, text size, color, and so on) that was present on the placeholder text is also applied to the text you enter.

If you create a blank page, any text that is inserted onto the page must be formatted with an appropriate font, color, or other text attribute. Like Word, FrontPage also provides you with the capability to align text.

REPLACING PLACEHOLDER TEXT

Replacing the placeholder text that the wizards and templates place on your text pages is just a matter of selecting the text and then typing your new text.

To replace placeholder text, follow these steps:

1. Open the page you want to edit in the Page view.

2. Select the placeholder text you want to replace on the page (see Figure 5.1).

Selected placeholder text

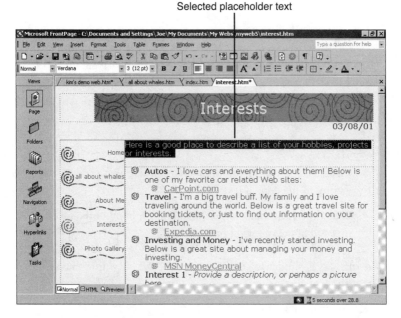

FIGURE 5.1
Select the placeholder text and then type your own text to replace it.

3. Type the text that replaces the placeholder text.

4. After you change the text on a particular page, be sure you save the changes; click the **Save** button on the toolbar.

INSERTING NEW TEXT

Inserting new text is a matter of positioning the insertion point (the mouse I-beam) on the page and then typing your new text. When you add new text to the page, the text is formatted using the default text attributes for the page (determined by the theme assigned to that page). This includes text formatting such as the font, size, and color of the text.

If you insert text onto a new page that does not have a theme assigned to it, the text is inserted in a Times New Roman default font. You can then modify the look of the text as needed.

COPYING, MOVING, AND DELETING TEXT

You can copy or cut text and then paste it to another location on the current page or switch to another page in the web and paste the text there. Follow these steps to copy and paste text:

1. Select the text you want to copy.

2. Select the **Edit** menu and select **Copy**.

3. Place the insertion point on the page where you want to place a copy of the copied text.

4. Select the **Edit** menu and select **Paste**. A copy of the text is inserted at the insertion point.

Moving text is similar to copying the text—the only difference is the use of the Cut command rather than Copy:

1. Select the text you want to move.

2. Select the **Edit** menu, and then select **Cut** to cut the text from its current position.

3. Place the insertion point on the page where you want to move the text.

4. Select the **Edit** menu and select **Paste**. The text is moved to the new location (defined by the insertion point).

TIP

> **Drag and Drop Your Text**   You can also use drag and drop
> to move text on a Web page. Select the text and, without
> releasing the mouse button, drag the insertion point to a
> new location. When you release the mouse button,
> FrontPage moves your text to the insertion point's new
> location.

To delete placeholder text or text that you've placed on a page, select
the text and press the **Delete** key on the keyboard.

CHANGING HOW THE TEXT LOOKS

You have complete control over the formatting attributes of the text on
the pages of your web. You can format text using the various buttons
on the FrontPage Formatting toolbar, or you can take advantage of the
text styles that are provided by the theme or template that you assign
to your Web page or pages.

USING THE FORMATTING TOOLBAR

The Formatting toolbar enables you to change the font, text size, text
attributes (such as bold and italic), and color of the font. In most
cases, it's a matter of selecting the text and then clicking the appropriate attribute button on the Formatting toolbar to change the look of the
text. Bold, italic, and underline work in this manner.

Other attributes, such as the font, font size, or font color, require that
you select the text and then select your formatting change from a list
or palette. For example, to change the font, select the text and then
select a new font using the Font drop-down box on the Formatting
toolbar. Font size is also controlled by a drop-down box on the
Formatting toolbar. Changing the color of selected text requires that
you choose a new color from a color palette.

To change the color of the text on a page, follow these steps:

1. Select the word or other text that you want to change the color of.

2. Click the **Font Color** drop-down button on the Formatting toolbar. The color palette appears (see Figure 5.2).

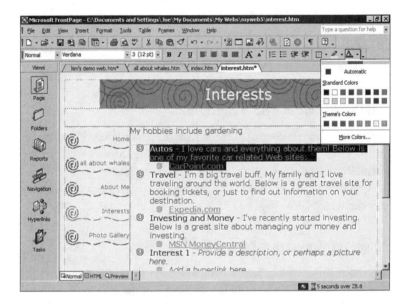

FIGURE 5.2
Changing text attributes such as color requires that you select the text and then choose the new attribute on the Formatting toolbar.

3. Choose a font color from the palette. The text color changes.

4. Click anywhere on the page to deselect the text.

CAUTION

Text Attribute Changes Override Theme Styles FrontPage relies heavily on styles to format the text on the pages in your web, especially if you've chosen a theme for your pages. When you select text and change the formatting using the buttons on the Formatting toolbar, these changes override the current style. In fact, even if you change the style of this modified text, the attributes provided by the new style also are overridden by your former formatting changes.

USING FRONTPAGE STYLES

A style is a grouping of formatting attributes identified by a style name. A style might include text-formatting attributes such as bold text, a particular font color, and a particular font size. Styles can also contain text alignment attributes such as center or right-align.

FrontPage provides several built-in styles from which you can choose. There are a series of heading styles, styles for bulleted and numbered lists, and a number of others. To use styles, you must understand how FrontPage views text on a Web page. Each line of text that is followed by a paragraph mark (placed at the end of the line or paragraph when you press the Enter key) is considered a separate paragraph. To assign a particular style to a text paragraph (whether it's a single line or several lines of text), all you have to do is place the insertion point somewhere in the text block.

To assign a built-in style to text on a page, follow these steps:

1. Place the insertion point into the paragraph you want to assign the style to.

2. Click the **Style** drop-down box on the Formatting toolbar.

3. Select a style from the drop-down list.

The style is assigned to your text paragraph.

You can also create your own text styles if you want. Follow these steps:

1. Select **Format** and then **Style** to open the Style dialog box (see Figure 5.3).

2. Click the **List** drop-down box under the currently listed styles and select **User-Defined Styles**.

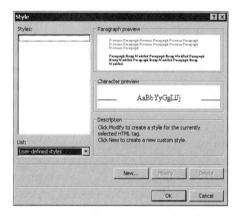

FIGURE 5.3
The Style dialog box is the starting place for creating, editing, and managing the styles for your pages.

3. To create the new style, click the **New** button. The New Style dialog box appears.

4. Type a name for your new style into the **Name** box.

5. Click the **Format** button on the bottom left of the New Style dialog box. Select **Font** to change the font attributes for style (the Font dialog box appears).

6. After completing your font attribute selections, click **OK** to return to the New Style dialog box. To include other attributes in the style, click the **Format** button again and select **Paragraph**, **Border**, or other style attributes as required.

7. When you have finished the formatting choices for the style, click **OK** to close the New Style dialog box and return to the Style dialog box. Your new style appears in the style list.

8. Click **OK** again to return to your page.

You can assign your new style to text on the page the same as you can any of the premade styles. Place the insertion point on the text and click the **Style** drop-down box on the Formatting toolbar. Select your style (which appears at the end of the style list).

CAUTION

> **Styles Are Not Shared by Different Pages**   When you cre-ate a FrontPage style for a particular page, it is good only on that page. You can't use it on any other pages—not even pages in the same web. You must re-create it for each page on which you want to use it.

ALIGNING TEXT

Another aspect of formatting text is aligning it on the page. The default alignment for new text on a Web page is left-justified. This means it aligns directly against the left margin of a page or against any shared borders that have been placed on the left side of a page. (Shared borders are discussed in Lesson 8, "Inserting Special FrontPage Components.")

The simplest way to align text on a page is using the alignment but-tons on the Formatting toolbar. First, place the insertion point in the text and then select one of the following alignment possibilities:

- **Left Justified**—The default justification for normal text, aligned on the left. Click the **Align Left** button on the Formatting toolbar.

- **Right Justified**—Text is aligned at the right margin. A ragged-left edge is present on text that is right-aligned. Click the **Align Right** button on the Formatting toolbar.

- **Center**—The text is centered between the left and right mar-gins of the page. Click the **Center** button on the Formatting toolbar.

CHANGING PAGE NAMES

When you create pages using the Web Wizards, default page names are assigned to the pages in the web. Often, you want to customize these page names to suit your own needs. Unfortunately, when you click one of the premade page banners placed at the top of the page, you will find that you cannot edit the text as you would regular text on the page. The banner does not allow you to select the text or place the insertion point on the banner.

For example, if you create a new web using the Personal Web Wizard, four pages are created for you: Home Page, Interests, Photo Album, and Favorites. The wizard automatically places page banners at the top of each page (more about page banners is covered in Lesson 6, "Working with Graphics in FrontPage"). If you want to change the text in the banner, you must change the page name itself. For example, if you want to change the Interests page's banner to read Hobbies, you must change the page's name.

To change the page name for a page in your web, follow these steps:

1. Click the **Navigation** icon on the Views bar to go to the Navigation view.

2. Right-click the page you want to rename and select **Rename** from the shortcut menu that appears (see Figure 5.4).

3. Type the new name for the page.

4. Click any other page in the web to deselect the **Name** box for the page that was edited.

In this lesson, you learned how to add, edit, and format text on your Web pages, including the creation of your own styles. You also learned to change the page names for pages in your web. In the next lesson, you learn how to work with graphics in FrontPage.

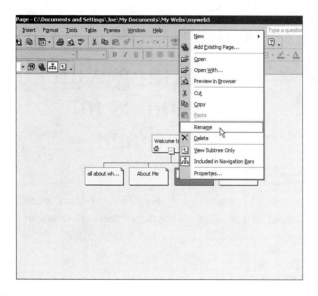

FIGURE 5.4

Change the page name of a page in the Navigation view.

LESSON 6

Working with Graphics in FrontPage

In this lesson, you learn how to insert pictures, clip art, and motion clips into your Web pages and save the graphical files as part of your web. You also learn how to preview pages in the web.

INSERTING PICTURES

FrontPage makes it easy for you to insert images, clip art, and special animated images into your Web pages. You can insert pictures that you download from the World Wide Web, scan with a scanner, or capture with a digital camera. You can also insert clip art and motion clips from the Clip Art Gallery.

You will find that FrontPage enables you to insert several picture file formats into your Web pages:

- CompuServe GIF (.gif)
- Encapsulated PostScript (.eps)
- Various paint programs (.pcx)
- Tagged Image File format (.tif)
- Windows bitmap (.bmp)
- JPEG File Interchange format (.jpg)

Inserting a picture onto a Web page is really just a matter of placing the insertion point at the appropriate position and then locating the picture file that you want to insert.

To insert a picture file, follow these steps:

1. Open the page (double-click it in the Navigation view) where you want to place the picture. You are in the Page view.

2. Place the insertion point where you want to place the graphic.

3. Select **Insert**, point at **Picture**, and select **From File** on the cascading menu. The Picture dialog box appears (see Figure 6.1).

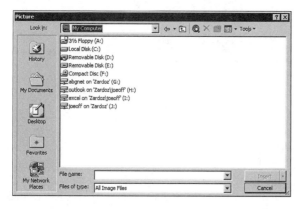

FIGURE 6.1
The Picture dialog box allows you to insert picture files into your Web pages.

4. Use the **Look In** drop-down list (near the top left of the dialog box) to locate the drive that contains the picture file, and double-click to open the folder that holds the file. After you locate the picture, click the file to select it.

5. Click **OK**, and the image is placed on your page (see Figure 6.2).

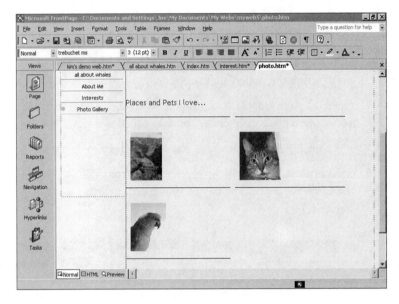

FIGURE 6.2
Pictures can add visual interest to your Web pages.

INSERTING CLIP ART

You can also insert any number of images from the Clip Art Gallery. Drawings of animals, computers, and even cartoons are available for you to use on your Web pages.

To insert clip art images, follow these steps:

1. Open the page (double-click it in the Navigation view) where you want to place the picture. You are in the Page view.

2. Place the insertion point where you want to place the clip art.

3. Select the **Insert** menu and point at **Picture**. Select **Clip Art** from the cascading menu. The Insert Clip Art task pane opens.

4. Type a subject or category (such as Animals) into the Search text box to view a set of images (see Figure 6.3).

FIGURE 6.3
Each Clip Art Gallery category provides a set of related images.

5. When you locate the image you want to use, click the image. A drop-down list appears, which contains several options for using that piece of clip art.

6. Click **Insert** on the list to place the image on your page.

INSERTING CLIP ART GALLERY MOTION CLIPS

The Clip Art Gallery also provides several motion clips that you can place on your Web pages. These motion clips are actually animated clip art. These animated images are activated when someone visits a page on your web that contains the animation.

Motion clips can add interest and excitement to your site. To insert a motion clip, follow these steps:

1. Open the page (double-click it in the Navigation view) where you want to place the picture. You are in the Page view.

2. Place the insertion point where you want to place the clip art.

3. Select the **Insert** menu and then point at **Picture**. Select **Clip Art** from the cascading menu. The Clip Art task pane opens.

4. Type in a subject (such as Clocks) under **Search Text**.

5. Check the **Movies** box under the **Results Should Be** pull-down menu. Then click the **Search** button.

CAUTION

> **Not All the Clip Categories Provide Motion Clips**   When you are looking for motion clips in the various Clip Art Gallery categories, you might find that a particular category does not provide any motion clips at all.

6. To preview a motion clip, click the clip's pop-up menu and click **Preview/Properties**. A Preview/Properties box appears, and the animation starts playing (see Figure 6.4).

FIGURE 6.4
*Motion clips can be previewed by clicking **Preview/Properties** before you insert the clips onto your Web pages.*

7. When you have finished previewing the motion clip, click the **Close** button in the preview's lower-right corner.

8. To insert a motion clip, click the image and then click **Insert** on the pop-up menu to place the image onto your page.

The motion clip appears as a static image on your Web page. You must preview the page to see the motion clip in action (see the section "Previewing Your Images" in this lesson for more information) .

SAVING THE IMAGE TO YOUR WEB

You might think that inserting a picture file, clip-art image, or motion clip onto a particular page makes that image part of your web—it is, after all, on one of the web's pages. Unfortunately, like inserting a new page into the Web (as covered in Lesson 4, "Working with Web Pages"), that's not the case. When you save the page where you inserted the image, you also have to save the image itself as a separate file that is placed with the other files held in the current Web folder. A Save Embedded Files dialog box appears after your save the page. Use this dialog box to save the images that you have placed on the page as separate Web files.

Web pages can't have graphics that are embedded on the pages. So, when you insert a graphic onto a FrontPage Web page, you are actually setting up a link between the page and the graphic that you inserted. When you view Web pages on the World Wide Web using your Web browser, the pictures you see are linked to the page that you open in your browser.

Another thing you should be aware of is that when the inserted image (picture, clip art, and so on) is saved to the web, it is saved in a file format that is best for viewing on Web pages. Files in any format other than .gif or .jpg are converted to .gif files when you save them to the web. Web pages typically contain .gif and .jpg files because these two file formats provide good resolution and color in a fairly compact file size.

To save a page image as part of the web, follow these steps:

1. With the page open in the Page view, click the **Save** button on the toolbar. The Save Embedded Files dialog box appears (see Figure 6.5).

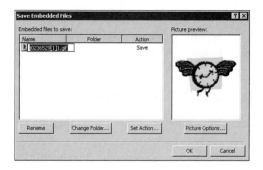

FIGURE 6.5
Embedded graphics must be saved as separate files in the Web folder.

2. A new name for the file is provided (based on the original filename of the image) and the image is saved as a .gif file by default (if it's not already a .jpg). Click **OK** to save the file.

The image file is now part of the web. The new file created in step 2 is placed in your Web folder.

TIP

> **Save Photos As .jpg Files**   The Save Embedded Files dialog box saves all inserted images that are not .jpg files as .gif files by default. In the case of scanned photos or photos taken with a digital camera that are not .jpg files when you insert them, you might want to force FrontPage to save them as .jpg files rather than .gif files. Photos look better on the Web when saved as .jpg. In the Save Embedded Files dialog box, select the photo's filename, and then click the **Picture Options** button. In the Picture Options dialog box that appears, click the **JPEG** option button, and then click OK. Now when you save the file it is saved in the .jpg format.

CAUTION

**The Save As Dialog Box Appears If the Page Hasn't Been
Saved**   When you click the **Save** button to save an
embedded image on a page, the Save As dialog box
appears if the page itself hasn't been saved before.
Provide a name and save the page. Then, the Save
Embedded Files dialog box appears, and you can save
the image file to the web.

SIZING THE IMAGE

You can size any image you place on a page. As you size an image,
you will find that it affects the text below the image. The larger you
make the picture, the more the text is moved down the page.

To size an image, follow these steps:

1. Click the image to select it.

2. Place the mouse pointer on any of the sizing handles that
   appear around the image. The mouse pointer becomes a two-
   headed arrow.

3. Drag to increase or decrease the size of the image (see
   Figure 6.6). Release the mouse when you have finished sizing the image.

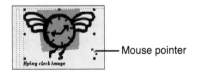 —— Mouse pointer

FIGURE 6.6
Use the sizing handles to increase or decrease the size of your image.

TIP

> **Maintain the Image's Height/Width Ratio**   Use the sizing handles on the corners of the image and drag diagonally to maintain the image's height/width ratio. This keeps the image from looking distorted.

ALIGNING THE IMAGE

You can also align your images on the page. The simplest way to align a graphic is using the alignment buttons on the Formatting toolbar. For example, to place an image on the center of the page, click the **Center** button on the toolbar.

When you use the Formatting toolbar buttons, however, you are changing only the position of the image; you are not changing how text on the page wraps around the image. The default setting for how text relates to a picture is for text not to wrap around the image.

To change the position of an image in relation to surrounding text, you must use settings found in the Picture Properties dialog box.

To change image alignment and how text wraps around the image, follow these steps:

1. Right-click the image and select **Picture Properties** from the shortcut menu. The Picture Properties dialog box appears.

2. Click the **Appearance** tab on the Picture Properties dialog box. Picture alignment and text wrapping are controlled by the Alignment drop-down box and the Wrapping Style boxes (see Figure 6.7).

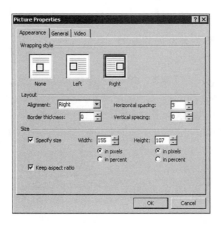

FIGURE 6.7
Use the Alignment box and the Wrapping Style boxes on the Appearance tab to control the alignment of a picture and how text wraps around it.

3. The first time you go to the Appearance tab, the setting in the Alignment box is Default. Default means that the picture is aligned where you inserted it (normally on the left side of the page) and text does not wrap around the picture.

4. To change the position of the picture and how text wraps around the picture, click one of the Wrapping Style boxes to make one of the following selections:

   • **Left**—This aligns the picture on the left of the page and allows text to wrap around the image on the right.

   • **None**—This enables you to place text on both the left and right side of the image. (It does not center the image relative to the page, but places the image in the center of the text.)

   • **Right**—This places the image on the right of the page and allows text to wrap around the left side of the picture.

5. After you make your alignment selection, click **OK** to close the Picture Properties dialog box.

You are returned to your page. You can now insert text on the page so that it wraps around the picture (depending on which of the alignment options you chose).

If you want to place a border around a particular picture, open the Picture Properties dialog box for that picture and click the **Appearance** tab. Use the **Border Thickness** box to set a thickness for a border around the picture. Click **OK** to close the dialog box after you've set the border thickness.

PREVIEWING YOUR IMAGES

When you work with pictures and graphics on a page, it's nice to be able to take a quick look at how they appear when your pages are viewed on the World Wide Web. This is particularly useful if you've placed motion clips on your pages and want to see how they look when the animations are playing.

When you are in Page view, you can quickly preview a particular page and the elements you have placed on that page. Click the **Preview** tab at the bottom of the page window. The page as it appears in a Web browser displays in the Preview mode (see Figure 6.8).

To return to your page so that you can edit it, click the **Normal** tab.

The Preview mode provides a quick view of how things will appear on the World Wide Web. The test, however, is to view pages in a Web browser, which gives you a true picture of how the site will look. Keep in mind, however, that Web pages will look decidedly different in different Web browsers. FrontPage is set up to produce webs that work well when viewed with Microsoft Internet Explorer. If your audience is going to use other Web browsers (and they will if your audience is everyone on the Internet), you should test your site using other browsers, such as Netscape Navigator.

FIGURE 6.8
Previewing your pages enables you to see how graphics (especially motion clips) look on the World Wide Web.

In this lesson, you learned how to place picture files, clip art, and motion clips on your pages. You also learned how to save the pictures to the web and align the pictures on the page. In the next lesson, you learn how to insert sounds and videos into your Web pages.

LESSON 7

Adding Sounds and Video to Web Pages

In this lesson, you learn how to insert sounds and videos onto your Web pages and preview this special Web content.

WORKING WITH SOUNDS

FrontPage makes it easy for you to add sound to your Web pages. You actually have two alternatives for adding sound files. You can add the sound as an object on the Web page that can then be played by a user viewing your Web page, or you can add sounds to a page as a background file; when the page is viewed the sound will play. We will take a look at both possibilities in this lesson.

Sound files come in a number of different file formats and FrontPage embraces most sound file formats. Some of the most common sound file types are

- WAVE (.wav) —This is one of the most common sound file types.
- MIDI (.mid)
- AIFF (.aif)
- AU (.au or .snd)
- RealAudio (.ram)

Although each of these file types can be used to add sounds to your Web pages, you can't really assume that all users viewing your Web page will have the capability to play all sound types. Sticking to common sound file types such as WAVE and MIDI should assure that most users can play the sounds you place on your web.

FrontPage actually offers a number of sound files that are part of the Clip Art library. You can insert them as you would any Clip Art file (as discussed in Lesson 6, "Working with Graphics in FrontPage"). Adding Clip Art sound files to a page actually assigns the Clip Art sound to the Web page. When the page is opened, the sound plays automatically. We will discuss how you can assign any sound file to a Web page later in this lesson.

If you have a microphone, you can also create your own sound files using the Windows Sound Recorder (this enables you to create your own WAVE files). A large number of sound files are also available on the World Wide Web and can be downloaded using your Web browser.

Although adding sound files from the Clip Art library does add audio content to your Web pages, you might find that there are a limited number of sound files available (and so you may want to create your own or browse the Web for noncopyrighted files that you can use). A great way to add sound to Web pages so that the user viewing your Web page has the option of playing (or not playing) the sound file is to assign the sound to a hover button.

CAUTION

> **Not All Sound Files Are Free**   When you download sound files from the Web, many of these sound files are actually copyrighted, particularly those that are sound clips from movies or television programs. Be sure that you have permission to use a sound file before you make it part of your Web site.

ADDING SOUND TO A HOVER BUTTON

As already mentioned, one way to add a sound file to a Web page is to add the sound so that a user has the option of playing the sound file. You do this by first inserting a hover button onto the Web page. You can then assign the sound file to the hover button. When a user clicks on the hover button the sound will play.

First you need to insert the hover button, then you can assign the sound to the button; follow these steps:

1. Open the page (double-click it in the Navigation view) where you want to place the hover button. You are in the Page view.

2. Place the insertion point where you want to place the hover button.

3. Select **Insert**, and then **Web Component**. The Insert Web Component dialog box appears (see Figure 7.1).

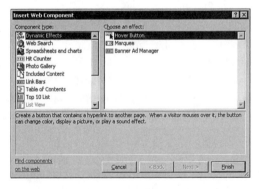

FIGURE 7.1
The Insert Web Component dialog box enables you to insert a hover button.

4. Select **Dynamic Effects** in the Component type box. Then select **Hover Button** in the Choose an Effect box.

5. Click **Finish**. The Hover Button Properties dialog box appears (see Figure 7.2).

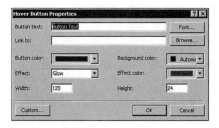

FIGURE 7.2
Link your sound file to the hover button in the Hover Button Properties dialog box.

6. In the Button text box of the dialog box, type the text you want to place on the hover button.

7. To assign the sound to the hover button, click in the Link To box and then click the **Browse** button. The Select Hover Button dialog box opens.

8. Use the Select Hover Button dialog box to locate the sound file on your computer's hard drive. Select the sound file and then click the **OK** button. You are returned to the Hover Button Properties dialog box.

9. Select any other hover button properties, such as the Button color or an Effect for the button. Click **OK** when you are ready to place the button on the page.

The hover button is placed on your Web page. To actually test the hover button (to be sure it plays the correct sound file), preview the page in your Web browser. Select **File**, then **Preview in Browser**. When the Preview in Browser dialog box opens, click **Preview**.

The page opens in your default Web browser (see Figure 7.3). Click on the hover button you created. If you used a WAVE file, the Windows Media Player (or your default WAVE file player) will open and play the sound file. Close the player and then close the browser window to return to FrontPage.

FIGURE 7.3
Preview the page in your Web browser to be sure the hover button plays the sound.

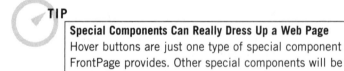

TIP

> **Special Components Can Really Dress Up a Web Page**
> Hover buttons are just one type of special component FrontPage provides. Other special components will be discussed in Lesson 8, "Inserting Special FrontPage Components."

Adding Page Background Sounds

You can also assign a sound file to a Web page. The sound file plays automatically when the page is opened in a Web browser. Adding background sounds is an excellent way to customize your Web site. As already mentioned, you can use the Insert menu to insert a Clip Art library sound on your Web page. These sounds then play when you

open the Web page. If you want to assign other sound files (specifi-
cally those that you create), you need to specify the sound file on the
Web page's Properties dialog box.

To assign a background sound to a Web page, follow these steps:

1. Open the page (double-click it in the Navigation view) to which
   you want to assign the sound file. You are in the Page view.

2. Select the **File** menu and then select **Properties**. The Page
   Properties dialog box appears (see Figure 7.4).

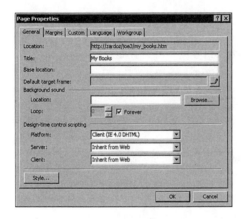

FIGURE 7.4
Use the Page Properties dialog box to assign a sound file to the page.

3. Click in the Location box of the Page Properties dialog box
   and then click the **Browse** button. The Background Sound
   dialog box appears.

4. Use the Background Sound dialog box to locate the sound
   file you will use. Then select the file in the dialog box and
   click **Open**. The sound file's location and name are placed in
   the Location dialog box.

5. If you want the sound to loop (play) continuously, be sure the
   Forever check box is selected. If you only want the sound

file to loop a certain number of times, clear the Forever check box and then use the Loop spin dial to set the number of times the sound file should play.

   6. After setting the loop number, click **OK**.

The sound file is assigned to the page. Preview the page in your Web browser as detailed at the end of the previous section. The sound should play when the page opens and should "loop" the number of times that you specified.

INSERTING VIDEO FILES ONTO A WEB PAGE

Another way to add interest to a Web page, and supply information in an alternative format, is to insert a video file onto a Web page. FrontPage provides a number of animated video clips that you can add to your Web pages (just as you add any clip art). However, you may also want to add video content that shows how a particular product that you sell works, or video that you shoot yourself, such as video clips from that fantastic beach vacation you just took in the islands.

Video files come in a number of different formats, such as .avi (the Windows default video format), .mpg, and .mov. Windows Media Player (typically the default video player for Windows-based computers) plays a number of different file formats. You should test your video file for playback before you use it on your Web page.

To insert a video file onto a Web page, follow these steps:

   1. Open the page (double-click it in the Navigation view) to which you want to assign the sound file. You are in the Page view.

   2. Select **Insert**, then point at **Picture**, then select **Video**. The Video dialog box appears.

   3. Use the Video dialog box to locate your video file; then select the file. Click **Open** to insert the video file and close the dialog box.

4. You can setup the video file so that it runs when the Web page is opened or when the user viewing your Web page places their mouse on the video box on the Web page. Select the video box, and then right-click. Select **Picture Properties** on the shortcut menu that appears.

5. The Picture Properties dialog box appears (see Figure 7.5).

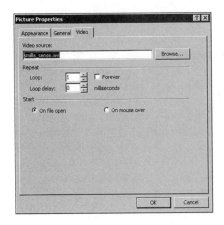

FIGURE 7.5
Use the Picture Properties dialog box to set when the video will play.

6. If you want the video to play when a user places the mouse on it, click the **On Mouse Over** option button.

7. Click **OK** to close the dialog box.

To preview the page in your Web browser, select **File**, then **Preview in Browser**. When the Preview in Browser dialog box opens, click **Preview**.

The page opens in your default Web browser. To watch the video play, place your mouse on the video. When you are done previewing the video, close the browser window to return to FrontPage.

In this lesson, you learned how to assign a sound file to a hover button and to a Web page. You also learned how to place a video on a Web page and have it play when the mouse is placed on it. In the next lesson, you learn how to insert FrontPage special components on your Web pages.

LESSON 8
Inserting Special FrontPage Components

In this lesson, you learn how to insert special FrontPage components such as navigation bars, page banners, shared borders, and hit counters.

UNDERSTANDING SPECIAL COMPONENTS

FrontPage provides several special elements, called *components*, that you can place on your Web pages. These components are designed to take the place of sophisticated elements such as navigation bars and hit counters that you would normally have to create using the HTML coding language.

Many special components are available in FrontPage. Table 8.1 defines some of the commonly used components.

Table 8.1   FrontPage Special Components

Component	Purpose
Shared borders	A shared border is an area that is common to the pages in your web. Any item placed in a shared border appears on all the pages of the web.
Page banner	Displays the page name at the top of the page. Page banners use the text attributes and pictures of a theme assigned to that page. Page banners placed in shared borders display the page name of every page in the web.

Table 8.1   (continued)

Component	Purpose
Navigation bar	A set of text or graphics that provides hyperlinks to the other pages in a Web site. A navigation bar placed in a shared border is displayed on all the pages in the web.
Hit counters	A page component that appears as a numbered counter and keeps count of the number of visits (called *hits*) to your Web site.

Normally, the creation of items such as those mentioned in Table 8.1 requires a good understanding of HTML programming and is usually the sign of a fairly sophisticated Web site. However, FrontPage enables you to place very complex components (complex in a programming sense) on your Web pages by taking advantage of the options available on the Insert menu.

CAUTION

> **The FrontPage Extensions Must Be Installed on the Web Server If You Use Special Components**   The FrontPage special components require that FrontPage extensions be installed on the Web server that hosts your web. You should talk to your Internet service provider before publishing your web to their web server. If they do not use the FrontPage extensions, you should forgo the use of special components in your web if you want it to function correctly on the server.

USING SHARED BORDERS

Shared borders enable you to create an area on the top, bottom, left, or right of a page that can be shared by all the pages in the Web site. Shared borders are similar to headers and footers used in Microsoft Word where you want information of some type to appear on all the pages of a document. In FrontPage, this enables you to put items such as navigation bars or page banners in the shared border area so that they appear on all the pages. This means that you have to insert the component (such as a navigation bar) into the shared border area on only one of the pages in the web, and the component appears on all the pages in the web (in the shared border area).

If you've used any of the Web Wizards to create your web, you've already seen the application of shared borders. For example, webs created using the Personal Web Wizard automatically place shared borders on the left and top of the pages in the web.

To insert shared borders on your Web pages or to modify the current shared borders, follow these steps:

1. Open one of the pages in your web (double-click it in the Navigation view).

2. Select the **Format** menu and then select **Shared Borders**. The Shared Borders dialog box appears (see Figure 8.1).

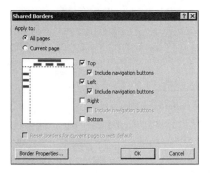

FIGURE 8.1
Set shared border parameters in the Shared Borders dialog box.

3. Option buttons at the top of the dialog box enable you to place the shared borders on **All Pages** or **Current Page**. For a web with consistent design, select the **All Pages** option button.

4. Click the appropriate check box for the location of the shared borders you want to place on the pages: **Top**, **Left**, **Right**, **Bottom**. You can check more than one box.

5. If you select Top or Left, you can also choose to have navigation buttons for the web automatically placed in the shared border area. Click the **Include Navigation Buttons** check box as needed to include navigation buttons.

6. When you have finished your selections, click **OK**.

Your shared borders appear on the page or pages of your web (depending on the selections you made in the Shared Borders dialog box). The shared border areas are excellent places to insert other special components, such as page banners, navigation bars, or even company logos or pictures. Any items you want to repeat on your Web pages can be placed in a shared border area. Figure 8.2 shows a Web page that has shared borders at the top and left of the page.

FIGURE 8.2
Shared borders enable you to place repeating elements on all the pages in your web.

CREATING PAGE BANNERS

Page banners provide a colorful heading for your pages that is consistent across the pages in a web. Page banners can consist of text that uses the font and colors of the theme selected for the web (if a theme was selected). Page banners can also consist of a graphical image with text that uses graphical elements, fonts, and colors from the current theme.

Page banners can be placed anywhere on the page (but are most useful at the top of the page as the main heading for that page). When a page banner is placed in a shared border area, it displays the appropriate page name for the current page and also appears on the other pages in the web. (The page name is the name assigned to the page in the Navigation view.)

To insert a page banner, follow these steps:

1. Open the page (double-click it in the Navigation view) where you want to place the page banner. If you plan on placing the banner in a shared border area, you can open any page in the web (displaying the shared border).

2. Place the insertion point where you want to place the banner. To place it in a shared border area, click within the shared border (placeholder text in the border area is selected).

3. Select **Insert**, **Page Banner**. The Page Banner Properties dialog box appears (see Figure 8.3).

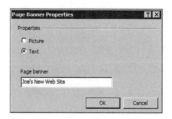

FIGURE 8.3
The Page Banner Properties dialog box enables you to insert a text or a graphical banner on your Web page.

4. Select the **Picture** or **Text** option button to determine the type of banner you create. If you select Picture, the banner will consist of a graphic containing the page's name. The banner format is based on the theme that has been selected for the web. If you use the Text option, the banner is inserted as regular text and can be formatted or aligned on the page as any other text element.

5. If you want to change the page banner text, select the text in the Page Banner Text box and type the new banner heading.

6. Click **OK** and the banner is placed on your page (see Figure 8.4).

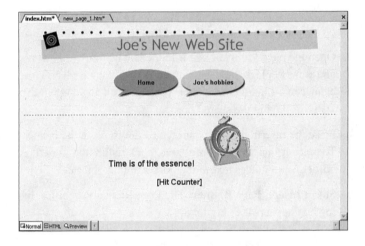

FIGURE 8.4
The new page banner appears on your Web page.

If you chose to place the page banner in a shared border, the new banner appears on each page in the web. If you want to modify a page banner, double-click the banner to open the Page Banner dialog box. You can remove a banner by selecting it and pressing the **Delete** key on the keyboard.

CAUTION

> **Changing the Banner Text Changes the Page Name**   If you decide to change the text for the banner in the Page Banner dialog box, this also changes the name of that particular page when you go to the Navigation view for the web.

INSERTING NAVIGATION BARS

Making it easy for visitors to your Web site to move between the pages in your web is a necessity (or they might not stay and view your site). Navigation links must be available on each page. Fortunately, FrontPage provides a way to quickly (and easily) place navigation links on your page in the form of navigation bars. Navigation bars— preprogrammed components that can be placed in the shared border area of your Web pages—provide direction-finding buttons that take you to the other pages in your web.

To insert a navigation bar into your web, follow these steps:

1. Open the page (double-click it in the Navigation view) where you want to place the navigation bar. If you plan on placing the navigation bar in a shared border area, you can open any page in the web (displaying the shared border).

2. Place the insertion point where you want to place the banner. To place it in a shared border area, click within the shared border (placeholder text in the border area is selected).

3. Select **Insert, Navigation**. The Insert Web Component dialog box appears (see Figure 8.5). Under Choose a Bar Type, you can select from several navigational bars (a description appears below each one as you click it). Choose a bar type and then an orientation (horizontal or vertical) for your links buttons. Press **Finish** when your selections are completed.

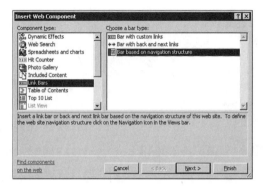

FIGURE 8.5
The Insert Web Component dialog box allows you to determine the type of navigation bar that is created on the pages.

4. After you press **Finish**, a Link Bar Properties box appears (see Figure 8.6). Option buttons are provided for you to choose the type of links (set up for you as hyperlinks) that can appear on the navigation bar. Select one of the buttons, depending on the navigation links you want to create:

- **Parent Level**—Provides a button or text link that takes you to the parent page of the current page.

- **Same Level**—Provides links to other pages in the web that are at the same level as the current page (when viewed in the Navigation view).

- **Back and Next**—Provides links to take you to the previous page and the next page.

- **Child Level**—Provides links to any child pages of the current page (pages shown below the current page in the Navigation view).

- **Top Level**—Provides links to any pages (including the home page) that are on the home page's level in the navigational structure of the web.

- **Child Pages Under Home**—Provides links to pages under Home. This is useful if you've divided your web into sections using section pages under Home in the navigational structure of the web.

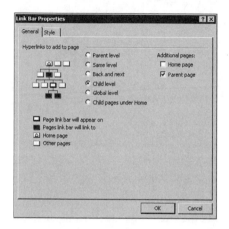

FIGURE 8.6
The Link Bar Properties box is where you choose the type of navigational structure you want on each page.

5. You can also choose to have links to your home page or parent page of the current page by selecting either the **Home Page** or **Parent Page** check box on the right of the dialog box. These links appear on the navigation bar in addition to the other links that you chose in step 4.

6. After making all your selections, click **OK**.

The navigation bar appears on the current page. Figure 8.7 shows a navigation bar that uses the colors and design elements of the current theme for the web (the Blocks theme). Buttons are chosen to show links to the home page of the web (the current page shown) and child pages of the current page (the other pages currently in the web).

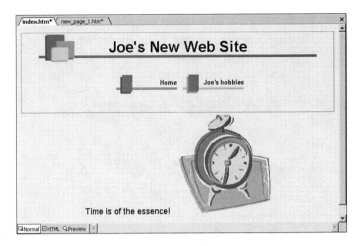

FIGURE 8.7
A navigation bar provides links to the other pages in your web.

If you want to edit the navigation bar, double-click it to open the
Navigation Bar dialog box. If you want to delete the navigation bar,
select it and press the **Delete** key.

INSERTING HIT COUNTERS

Another useful component that you might want to place on the home
page of your web is a hit counter. Hit counters show you and the visitors to your Web site how many hits (or visits) have been made to
your site. It's fun for visitors to see that their visit counts, literally, and
it's also important to see what kind of traffic your Web site is experi-
encing. Creating a hit counter normally requires pretty good knowl-
edge of HTML coding. Fortunately, FrontPage provides a number of
ready-made hit counters that you can insert as components.

To insert a FrontPage hit counter, follow these steps:

1. Open the home page for your site in the Page view. (The hit
   counter is typically placed on the main page for your site.)

2. Place the insertion point where you want to place the hit counter. Most sites place them directly below any text or graphics found on the home page of the Web site.

3. Select **Insert**, point at **Web Component**, and the Insert Web Component box appears (see Figure 8.8).

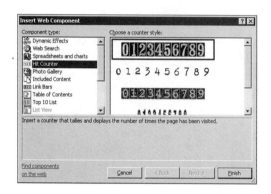

FIGURE 8.8
The Insert Web Component dialog box provides you with several hit counter styles.

4. Under Component Type choose **Hit Counter**. To the right, you see the Choose a Counter Style box. Select one of the hit counter styles from the dialog box.

5. Click **Finish**, and the Hit Counter Properties dialog box appears with your selection. Press **OK** to insert the selected hit counter onto your page.

The hit counter appears on your page as text (Hit Counter) enclosed in brackets. You cannot view the hit counter until you save the current web and publish it to a Web server that contains the Office server extension files. (Discuss the server extensions with your Internet service provider; the extension files must be on the ISP's Web server for special components such as the hit counter to work.)

In this lesson, you learned how to place shared borders, page banners, navigation bars, and other special components such as hit counters on your Web pages. In the next lesson, you learn how to work with hyperlinks.

Lesson 9
Working with Hyperlinks

In this lesson, you learn how to insert and manage hyperlinks on your Web pages.

UNDERSTANDING HYPERLINKS

An important aspect of creating Web pages is being able to insert hyperlinks onto the pages of your Web site. A *hyperlink* references another Web page on your site or another Web site on the World Wide Web. Hyperlinks are the main tool for navigating the World Wide Web.

For example, the navigation bars that you place on your Web pages so that visitors can navigate your Web site really consist of a list of ready-made hyperlinks to the pages on your site. (For more about navigation bars, see Lesson 8, "Inserting Special FrontPage Components.") You can also insert hyperlinks into your site that enable you to access other Web sites on the Web or send e-mail to a specific person.

Because FrontPage provides navigation bars that automatically provide hyperlinks to the pages in your web, you might wonder why you would ever create your own hyperlinks. First, if you want to create links to other Web sites on the Web, you must use hyperlinks. Also, if you place your Web pages on a Web server that does not recognize the Office Web server extensions, special FrontPage components such as the navigation bars do not function correctly; therefore, you must insert your own hyperlinks for the navigation of the pages in your site. You can then build a working site and post it to any Web server.

Hyperlinks can take the form of text or graphics. For example, a text line referencing a particular Web site can easily be turned into a hyperlink that takes you to that site. If you would rather link to another site using a graphic (such as a company logo), it can also be set up as a hyperlink. As with other Web page elements such as graphics, you should limit the number of hyperlinks that you place on the page. Avoiding cluttering up the page makes it easier for someone to use the hyperlinks to jump to other content on your Web.

FrontPage makes it easy for you to create hyperlinks to the pages in your own Web site using bookmarks. Bookmarks are discussed later in this lesson in "Using Bookmarks."

CREATING TEXT HYPERLINKS

Text hyperlinks are great for listing your favorite Web sites. You can create a list of text entries that describe the site to which the hyperlink connects. The descriptive text can be selected and then turned into a hyperlink for the described destination.

Another advantage of using text for hyperlinks is that the text appears in one color when viewed on the Web (blue, for example, is the default in FrontPage). When the link has been used (to go to the destination of the hyperlink) and the text is viewed again, it appears in a different color (violet is the default color for previously viewed hyperlinks in FrontPage). This makes it easy to keep track of the hyperlinks that have been used and those that have not.

To place a text hyperlink on a Web page, follow these steps:

1. Open the page (double-click it in the Navigation view) on which you want to place the hyperlink.

2. Type the text that will serve as the hyperlink. It can be the name of the site or any descriptive text you want.

3. Select the text you want to use as the hyperlink.

4. Select **Insert** and then select **Hyperlink**. The Insert Hyperlink dialog box appears (see Figure 9.1).

Use the Browse the Web button to find
an address to use as a link.

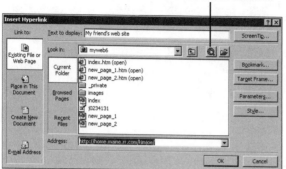

FIGURE 9.1
*The Insert Hyperlink dialog box enables you to create hyperlinks on your Web
pages.*

5. To create a link to a Web site, type the address of the site into
the Address box. This address typically takes the form
www.*nameofsite*.com. You can also select the address for the
link by using your Web browser. If you are connecting to
the Internet, you can click the **Browse the Web** button (to the
right of the Look In box). Your Web browser opens. Go to
the page you want to link to and click its address. Then
return to FrontPage. The page address appears in the Address box.

6. After you have the address in the Address box, click **OK**.

7. Click anywhere on the page to deselect the hyperlink text.

The text that was selected for the hyperlink is now underlined on your
Web page (see Figure 9.2).

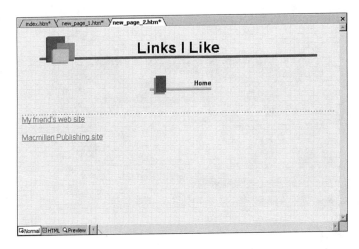

FIGURE 9.2
Your text hyperlink is underlined on the Web page.

TIP

> **How to Test External Hyperlinks**   If you want to test a
> hyperlink you've created that points to another Web site,
> open the page that contains the hyperlink. Be sure you
> are connected to the Internet, and then click the
> **Preview in Browser** button. This opens the current page
> in your Web browser. Click the hyperlink, and you should
> be taken to the site to which the hyperlink points.

CREATING GRAPHICAL HYPERLINKS

You can also make a graphic, such as a picture or clip art, a hyperlink
to a page in your Web site or to a page in another Web site. The
process of creating image hyperlinks is very straightforward and similar to the process of creating text hyperlinks.

To place a graphical hyperlink on a Web page, follow these steps:

  1. Open the page (double-click it in the Navigation view) on
     which you want to place the hyperlink.

2. Insert the picture or clip art you want to use as the hyperlink.

3. Select the graphic you want to use as the hyperlink.

4. Select **Insert, Hyperlink**. The Insert Hyperlink dialog box appears.

5. Type the address for the Web site you want to link to into the **Address** box. You can also select the address for the link by using your Web browser. If you are connecting to the Internet, you can click the **Browse the Web** button. Locate the page you want to link to and click its address. Then return to FrontPage. The page address appears in the Address box.

6. Click **OK** to return to the Web page.

The graphic is now a hyperlink to the address you provided in the Insert Hyperlink dialog box. Save the page and use your Web browser to test the link.

USING BOOKMARKS

If you want to create hyperlinks between pages on your own Web site or create links that jump to a particular position on a page (useful for very long pages that must be scrolled through), you might want to take advantage of bookmarks. A bookmark is a particular place or text on a page that you have marked—that is, you have made that spot on the page a bookmark. You can then use the bookmark to create a hyperlink that takes you to that bookmark.

To place a bookmark on a page, follow these steps:

1. In Page view, position the insertion point where you want to create a bookmark, or select the text or a graphic to which you want to assign the bookmark.

2. Select the **Insert** menu and then select **Bookmark**. The Bookmark dialog box opens (see Figure 9.3).

FIGURE 9.3
The Bookmark dialog box is where you name the new bookmark.

3. In the **Bookmark Name** box, type the name of the bookmark. If you selected text to serve as the bookmark, the
   selected text appears in the Bookmark Name box.

4. When you have finished naming your bookmark, click **OK**.

Selected text that has been designated as a bookmark has a dashed
line under it. If you designate a particular place on a page as a bookmark by inserting the insertion point, a small flag appears at that point
on the page.

Now that you've got a bookmark, you can create a hyperlink using it.
Follow these steps:

1. Go to the page where you want to place the hyperlink and
   select the text or graphic you want to use as the hyperlink.

2. Select **Insert**, **Hyperlink**. The Insert Hyperlink dialog box
   appears.

3. Click the **Bookmark** button and select the bookmark that
   will serve as the destination for the hyperlink.

4. Click **OK** to return to the Web page.

Now when you test the hyperlink, you should find that it takes you to the page in your web where you placed the bookmark.

To delete a bookmark that you no longer want or need, follow these steps:

1. Select the **Insert** menu and then select **Bookmark**.

2. In the Bookmark dialog box, select the bookmark you want to remove and click the **Clear** button.

3. Click **OK** to close the dialog box.

EDITING OR DELETING HYPERLINKS

You can also edit or delete the hyperlinks you place on your pages. You might think that by deleting a graphic or text that has been assigned a hyperlink, you also delete the hyperlink; in fact, you do. But in most cases, you probably want to keep the text or graphic on your Web page and change the hyperlink URL address or remove just the hyperlink attached to the text or graphic. Both of these tasks are handled in the Hyperlink dialog box.

Follow these steps to edit or remove a hyperlink:

1. Right-click the graphic or text that has been assigned the hyperlink. A shortcut menu appears.

2. Select **Hyperlink Properties** on the shortcut menu. The Edit Hyperlink dialog box opens.

3. To edit the hyperlink, select the address in the **Address** box and type a new address.

4. To delete the hyperlink, click the **Remove Link** button next to the address box. The address currently showing will have its link disconnected.

5. Click the **OK** button.

You will find that if the link was a text entry and you remove its hyperlinking capability, the text is no longer underlined. Edited hyperlinks can be tested by previewing the page in your Web browser.

In this lesson, you learned how to create and edit hyperlinks. You also learned to create bookmarks. In the next lesson, you will learn how to get help in FrontPage.

Lesson 10
Getting Help in Microsoft FrontPage

In this lesson, you learn how to access and use the Help system in Microsoft FrontPage.

Help: What's Available?

Microsoft FrontPage supplies a Help system that makes it easy for you to look up information on FrontPage commands and features as you work on your Websites and Web pages. Because every person is different, the Help system can be accessed in several ways. You can

- Ask a question in the Ask a Question box.

- Ask the Office Assistant for help.

- Get help on a particular element you see onscreen with the What's This? tool.

- Use the Contents, Answer Wizard, and Index tabs in the Help window to get help.

- Access the Office on the Web feature to view Web pages containing help information (if you are connected to the Internet).

Using the Ask a Question Box

The Ask a Question box is a new way to access the FrontPage Help system. It is also the easiest way to quickly get help. The Ask a Question box resides at the top right of the FrontPage window.

For example, if you are working in FrontPage and wish to view information on how to create a style, type **How do I add a banner?** into
the Ask a Question box. Then press the **Enter** key. A shortcut menu
appears below the Ask a Question box, as shown in Figure 10.1.

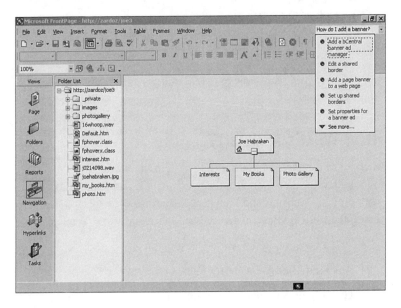

FIGURE 10.1
The Ask a Question box provides a list of Help topics based on your question.

To access one of the Help topics supplied on the shortcut menu, click
that particular topic. The Help window opens with topical matches for
that keyword or phrase displayed.

In the case of the "banner" question used in Figure 10.1 you could
select **Add a page banner to a Web page** from the shortcut menu that
appears. This opens the help window and displays help on how to add
a banner to a page. (see Figure 10.2).

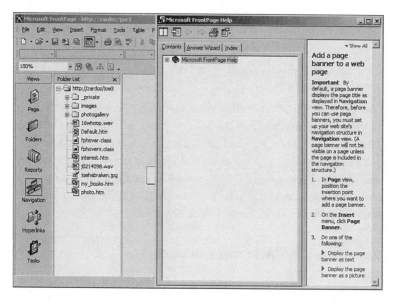

FIGURE 10.2
The Ask a Question box provides a quick way to access the Help window.

In the Help window, you can use the links provided to navigate the
Help system. You can also use the Contents, Answer Wizard, and
Index tabs to find additional information or look for new information
in the Help window. You learn more about these different Help window tabs later in this lesson.

USING THE OFFICE ASSISTANT

Another way to get help in Frontpage is to use the Office Assistant.
The Office Assistant supplies the same type of access to the Help system as the Ask a Question box. You ask the Office Assistant a question, and it supplies you with a list of possible answers that provide
links to various Help topics. The next two sections discuss how to use
the Office Assistant.

TURNING THE OFFICE ASSISTANT ON AND OFF

By default, the Office Assistant is off. To show the Office Assistant in your application window, select the **Help** menu and then select **Show the Office Assistant**.

You can also quickly hide the Office Assistant if you no longer want it in your application window. Right-click the Office Assistant and select **Hide**. If you want to get rid of the Office Assistant completely so it isn't activated when you select the Help feature, right-click the Office Assistant and select **Options**. Clear the **Use the Office Assistant** check box, and then click **OK**. You can always get the Office Assistant back by selecting **Help**, **Show Office Assistant**.

ASKING THE OFFICE ASSISTANT A QUESTION

When you click the Office Assistant, a balloon appears above it. Type a question into the text box. For example, you might type **How do I insert a new page?** for help adding a page to your Web. Click the **Search** button.

The Office Assistant provides a list of topics that reference Help topics in the Help system. Click the option that best describes what you're trying to do. The Help window appears, containing more detailed information. Use the Help window to get the exact information that you need.

Although not everyone likes the Office Assistant because having it enabled means that it is always sitting in your FrontPage window, it can be useful at times. For example, when you access particular features in FrontPage, the Office Assistant can automatically provide you with context-sensitive help on that particular feature. If you are brand new to Microsoft FrontPage, you might want to use the Office Assistant to help you learn the various features that FrontPage provides.

TIP

Select Your Own Office Assistant   Several different Office Assistants are available in Microsoft Office. To select your favorite, click the Office Assistant and select the **Options** button. On the Office Assistant dialog box that appears, select the **Gallery** tab. Click the **Next** button repeatedly to see the different Office Assistants that are available. When you locate the assistant you want to use, click **OK**.

USING THE HELP WINDOW

You can also forgo either the Type a Question box or the Office Assistant and get your help directly from the Help window. To directly access the Help window (the Office Assistant needs to be disabled), select **Help** and then the help command for the application you are using, such as **Microsoft FrontPage Help.** You can also press the **F1** key to make the Help window appear.

The Help window provides two panes. The pane on the left provides three tabs: Contents, Answer Wizard, and Index. The right pane of the Help window provides either help subject matter or links to different Help topics. It functions a great deal like a Web browser window. You click a link to a particular body of information and that information appears in the right pane.

The first thing that you should do is maximize the Help window by clicking its **Maximize** button. This makes it easier to locate and read the information that the Help system provides (see Figure 10.3).

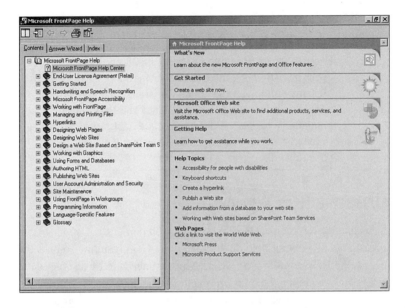

FIGURE 10.3
The Help window provides access to all the FrontPage help information.

When you first open the Help window, a group of links in the right pane provides you with access to information about new FrontPage features and other links, such as a link to Microsoft's Office Web site. Next, take a look at how you can take advantage of different ways to find information in the Help window: the Contents tab, the Answer Wizard tab, and the Index tab.

TIP

> **View the Help Window Tabs** If you don't see the differ-ent tabs in the Help window, click the **Show** button on the Help window toolbar.

USING THE CONTENTS TAB

The Contents tab of the Help system is a series of books you can open. Each book has one or more Help topics in it, which appear as pages or chapters. To select a Help topic from the Contents tab, follow these steps:

1. In the Help window, click the **Contents** tab on the left side of the Help window.

2. Find the book that describes, in broad terms, the subject for which you need help.

3. Double-click the book, and a list of Help topics appears below the book, as shown in Figure 10.4.

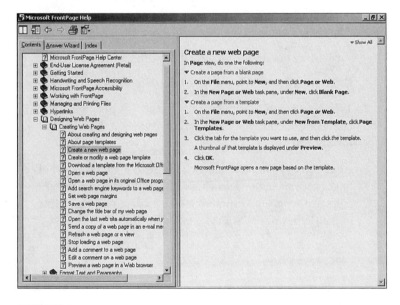

FIGURE 10.4
Use the Contents tab to browse through the various Help topics.

4. Click one of the pages (the pages contain a question mark) under a Help topic to display it in the right pane of the Help window.

5. Specific topic information will be condensed. Click a particular link to expand the information provided. When you finish reading a topic, select another topic on the Contents tab or click the Help window's **Close (x)** button to exit Help.

USING THE ANSWER WIZARD

Another way to get help in the Help window is to use the Answer Wizard. The Answer Wizard works the same as the Ask a Question box or the Office Assistant; you ask the wizard questions and it supplies you with a list of topics that relate to your question. You click one of the choices provided to view help in the Help window.

To get help using the Answer Wizard, follow these steps:

1. Click the **Answer Wizard** tab in the Help window.

2. Type your question into the What Would You Like to Do? box. For example, you might type the question, **How do I format text?**

3. After typing your question, click the **Search** button. A list of topics appears in the Select Topic to Display box. Select a particular topic, and its information appears in the right pane of the Help window, as shown in Figure 10.5.

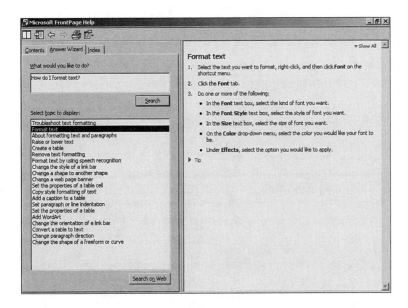

FIGURE 10.5
Search for help in the Help window using the Answer Wizard tab.

TIP

> **Print Help**   If you want to print information provided in the Help window, click the **Print** icon on the Help toolbar.

USING THE INDEX

The Index is an alphabetical listing of every Help topic available. It's like an index in a book.

Follow these steps to use the index:

1. In the Help window, click the **Index** tab.

2. Type the first few letters of the topic for which you are looking. The Or Choose Keywords box jumps quickly to a keyword that contains the characters you have typed.

3. Double-click the appropriate keyword in the keywords box. Topics for that keyword appear in the Choose a Topic box.

4. Click a topic to view help in the right pane of the Help window (see Figure 10.6).

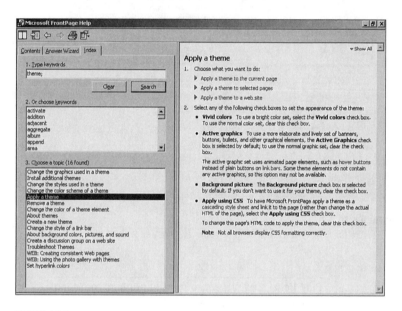

FIGURE 10.6
Use the Index tab to get help in the Help window.

TIP

Navigation Help Topics   You can move from topic to topic in the right pane of the Help window by clicking the various links that are provided there. Some topics are collapsed. Click the triangle next to the topic to expand the topic and view the help provided.

GETTING HELP WITH SCREEN ELEMENTS

If you wonder about the function of a particular button or tool on the Fronpage screen, wonder no more. Just follow these steps to learn about this part of Help:

1. Select **Help** and then **What's This?** or press **Shift+F1**. The mouse pointer changes to an arrow with a question mark.

2. Click the screen element for which you want help. A box appears explaining the element.

TIP

> **Take Advantage of ScreenTips**   Another Help feature provided by the Office applications is the ScreenTip. All the buttons on the different toolbars provided by FrontPage have a ScreenTip. Place the mouse on a particular button or icon, and the name of the item (which often helps you determine its function) appears in a ScreenTip.

In this lesson you learned how to access the FrontPage Help system. In the next lesson you will learn how to use FrontPage themes.

LESSON 11
Using FrontPage Themes

In this lesson, you learn how to use the FrontPage Themes and add horizontal lines to your Web pages.

WHAT ARE FRONTPAGE THEMES?

So far, we've concentrated on the individual elements of your Web pages such as text, pictures, FrontPage components, and hyperlinks. And while we've looked at how you can format text and add pictures, sounds, and videos to a Web page, we have not discussed how to create a Web site with a unified "look and feel."

FrontPage themes provide you with a specific look for your entire Web site. A specific theme controls the fonts, page layout, color scheme, and formatting for navigation bars and banners. Figure 11.1 shows a Web page formatted with the Nature theme (one of the many themes provided by FrontPage).

You may have already been introduced to FrontPage themes if you used a wizard, such as the Corporate Presence Wizard, to create your Web site. This wizard asks you to choose a theme during the Web creation process. If you created a blank Web page or used the Personal Web Wizard, you've only experienced the FrontPage default Straight Edge theme. There are a number of themes from which to choose, each with its own distinctive look.

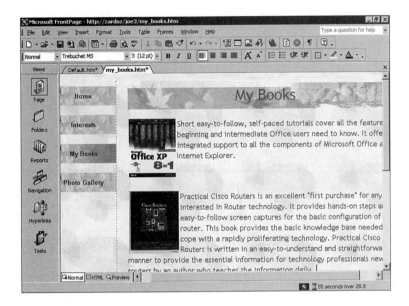

FIGURE 11.1
FrontPage themes add color, images, and interest to your Web pages.

You can assign a theme to your entire Web site or you can assign a theme to an individual page (or pages). Remember that when you assign a theme to a Web page or the Web site that all the existing formatting on your Web page or pages will be replaced.

Selecting a Theme for the Web Site

As already mentioned, you can assign a theme to the entire Web site (for a completely unified look and layout) or you can assign themes to individual pages or groups of selected pages. Let's take a look at how to assign a theme to all the pages in a Web site:

1. In the Navigation or Page view, select the **Format** menu and then select **Theme**. The Themes dialog box appears (see Figure 11.2).

FIGURE 11.2
The Themes dialog box gives you access to all the FrontPage themes.

2. If necessary, select the **All Pages** option button.

3. To choose your theme, scroll through the themes in the **Theme** scroll box. Select a particular theme to see a preview of the theme in the Sample of Theme box in the dialog box.

4. When you have found the theme you want to use for your Web site, select it.

5. You have several options related to the theme that appear in the lower left of the themes dialog box. These check boxes control the following attributes:

   - **Vivid colors**: Select this check box to use a more vivid color set with the theme.

   - **Active graphics**: This setting provides more elaborate buttons, bullets, and banners (active graphics using animated items on the page). Checked by default, clear this check box to use a set of non-animated graphics.

   - **Background picture**: Selected by default, clear this check box if you do not want to use the theme's background graphic on your Web page.

- **Apply using CSS**: FrontPage themes automatically change the HTML code of your pages. To have the theme attached as a style sheet to your Web page, select this check box.

6. After making your selections in the check boxes, click **OK**.

CAUTION

Not All Web Browsers Can Handle CSS Attached Style Pages   Not all Web browsers can view your Web theme correctly if you use the Apply Using CSS option. In most cases, you should go with the default and allow the theme to become part of the HTML code for the Web page.

The theme is assigned to all the pages in the Web site. To view a particular page, double-click the page in Navigation view.

SELECTING A THEME FOR A PAGE OR PAGES

Selecting a theme for an individual Web page or a group of pages in your Web site is similar to assigning a theme to your entire FrontPage Web site. If you want to select specific pages (rather than just one page), you can select the pages using the Folder list. Follow these steps to select a specific page:

1. In Navigation view, double-click the page to which you want to assign the theme. If you want to assign the theme to multiple pages, select **View**, and then **Folder** list. In the Folder list, click on the first page to which you want to assign the theme. To select additional pages, hold down the Ctrl key, and then click on the appropriate file names. Figure 11.3 shows the folder list and two selected pages.

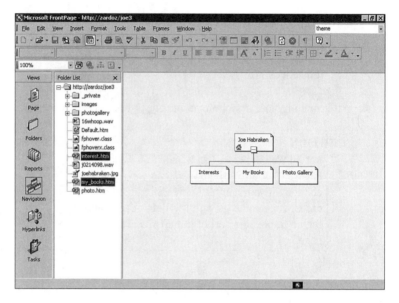

FIGURE 11.3
Use the Folder list to select multiple pages when assigning a theme.

2. Select the **Format** menu and then select **Theme**. The Themes dialog box appears.

3. Choose the **Selected Pages** option button.

4. Modify the settings for the theme using the check boxes (as discussed in the previous section).

5. Click **OK** to assign the theme to the page or pages.

You can open the selected pages from Navigation view to see how the new theme has affected their layout.

Modifying a Theme

You can also modify a theme. You can change the theme's colors, background picture, and the font used.

To modify a theme, follow these steps:

1. To open the Themes dialog box (to assign a theme to a page, Web site, or selected pages), select **Format**, then **Themes**.

2. In the Themes dialog box, click the **Modify** button. Colors, Graphics, and Text buttons appear (see Figure 11.4).

FIGURE 11.4
You can modify the attributes of a theme using the Colors, graphics, and text buttons.

3. To modify the colors used by the theme, click the **Colors** button. The Modify Theme dialog box appears (see Figure 11.5).

4. Select a new color scheme from the list provided.

5. (Optional) If you want to select the color scheme from the color wheel, select the **Color Wheel** tab in the dialog box. Click an area of the color wheel to select a new color scheme.

6. (Optional) If you want to assign a new color to each element on the page, select the **Custom** tab. Use the drop-down list to select a part of the page (such as the background or banner text) and then use the Color drop-down box to select a new color.

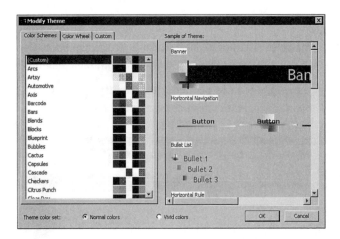

FIGURE 11.5
Choose a new color scheme for the theme.

7. When you have finished selecting a new color scheme, click **OK**. You are returned to the Themes dialog box.

8. To select a different background picture for the theme, click the **Graphics** button. The Modify Theme dialog box appears. Use the **Browse** button to locate and select a new background graphic for the theme (you can use any graphics file, including scanned images). Click **OK** to return to the Themes dialog box.

9. To select a new font for the theme, click the **Text** button. The Modify Theme dialog box appears. Use the Font list to select a new font for the theme, and then click **OK**.

10. When you have finished modifying the theme, click **OK**.

The new theme attributes are assigned to your Web page or pages.

USING HORIZONTAL LINES

While not one of the design elements provided by a FrontPage theme, you can add interest to your Web pages (and divide a particular Web page into different areas) by inserting horizontal lines. To insert a horizontal line on a page, follow these steps:

1. Go to Page view by clicking the **Page** icon on the Views bar.

2. Place the insertion point where you want to place the horizontal line.

3. Select the **Insert** menu, then select **Horizontal Line**. A horizontal line is placed at the insertion point.

If you are using a theme on the page (or for the entire Web site), you won't be able to modify the attributes of the line, such as color and thickness. This is controlled by the theme.

If you are not using a theme, you can easily modify the line. Right-click on it and select **Horizontal Line Properties** from the shortcut menu that appears.

The Horizontal Line Properties dialog box appears (see Figure 11.6). Use the Width and Height spinner boxes to changes these line attributes. You can select a new color for the line using the Color drop-down box. When you have finished changing the line's properties, click **OK**.

FIGURE 11.6
If you aren't using a theme, you can change the attributes of your horizontal lines.

In this lesson, you learned how to apply and modify FrontPage themes. You also learned how to insert horizontal lines on your Web pages. In the next lesson, you will learn how to create special forms for your Web pages.

LESSON 12
Creating Special Forms for Your Web

In this lesson, you learn how to create input forms on your Web pages.

UNDERSTANDING WEB FORMS

Although you probably have a feel for how a FrontPage web uses text and pictures to supply different kinds of information to visitors of your site, you might not know that you can design your site to request information from those visitors. FrontPage provides you with the capability to create various input forms that can be placed on your Web pages for use by your site visitors. This makes it easy for you to gather a variety of information. For example, on a personal Web, you can ask visitors to vote Yes or No on whether they like your site. On a corporate site, you can ask visitors interested in your products to provide their names and addresses so they can receive special offers or a catalog from your company.

The forms you create can be a combination of text boxes, radio buttons, check boxes, and drop-down lists that provide a set of choices for visitors. Before creating the form, however, you should decide what kind of information you want to collect, which definitely affects how the form looks and the type of input fields (text boxes versus check boxes) you place on the form. Figure 12.1 shows some of the input field types you can place on a form.

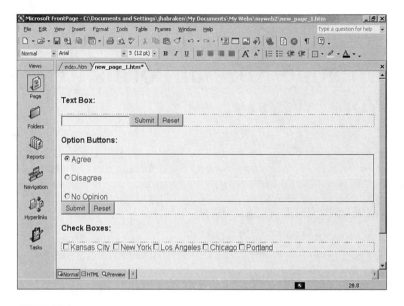

FIGURE 12.1
Your input forms can use different kinds of fields to gather information from visitors to your Web page.

CREATING A WEB FORM

The forms you create can be as simple or as complex as your need dictates. You can create a form that consists of just one text box that requests visitors to provide their e-mail addresses. Or, you can design a complex form that uses different field types, such as check boxes or drop-down lists.

How you begin the form creation process depends on how complex you want to make the form. If you are planning on making a form with a number of different input fields, your best bet is to insert a form on a page, and then insert the various input fields (such as radio buttons, text boxes, and so on) as required.

To place a blank form on a Web page, follow these steps:

1. Open the page (double-click it in Navigation view) where you want to place the form.

2. Place the insertion point where you want to create the form.

3. Select the **Insert** menu, and then point at **Form**. From the cascading menu, select **Form**. The blank form is placed on your page (see Figure 12.2).

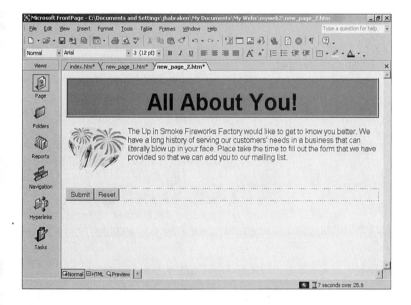

FIGURE 12.2
The blank form consists of a form box and Submit and Reset buttons.

The blank form provides Submit and Reset buttons and a workspace that you can use to insert the various form field types that receive input from visitors to your site. The next step in the process is to insert those input fields.

Inserting Form Fields

Form fields are the various text boxes, check boxes, or other items that you place on the form to gather information. FrontPage provides a number of different form field types. Table 12.1 lists some commonly used form field types and how you might use them in a form.

Table 12.1   Field Types for Your Forms

Field Type	Purpose
Text box	Use when requesting a single line of information, such as an e-mail address from a visitor.
Text area	Use when providing room for multiple lines of text in a scroll box format.
Check box	Use when providing a number of different options, where one or more options may be applicable.
Option button	Use when providing several choices and only one selection is required.
Drop-down box	Use when providing choices where one selection from menu is needed and there are space constraints (a drop-down menu takes up less space than several check boxes or radio buttons).

To place an input field in your form, follow these steps:

1. Place the insertion point in the form where you want to add the new input field. (You also can make room for fields by pressing the **Enter** key several times to move the Submit and Reset buttons down in the blank form.)

2. If you need label text to describe the input field, type the text in the form box. (For instance, if you are going to place a text box in the form for an e-mail address, you might want to type **E-mail Address** in the blank form, and then insert the field.)

3. To insert the field, select the **Insert** menu, and then point at **Form**. From the cascading menu, select the field you want to insert, such as **Text Box**.

The field appears in your form at the insertion point. Figure 12.3 shows a form in which descriptive text was inserted in a form, and then text fields were added as outlined in step 3. If you place a field in the wrong place or decide you don't want to use a particular field type, select the field on the page, and then press the **Delete** key to remove it.

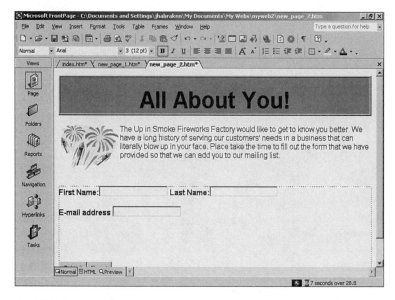

FIGURE 12.3
You can place descriptive text for the fields you insert in the form box.

As you can see, inserting the different field types into the form is very straightforward. The only field type that requires some extra work is the drop-down menu. After inserting it, you must provide the menu choices that appear on the menu. Follow these steps:

1. Insert a drop-down box field onto your form (**Insert**, **Form**, then **Drop-Down Box**).

2. Right-click the Drop-Down Box field (on your Web page) and select **Form Field Properties** from the shortcut menu. The Drop-Down Box Properties dialog box appears.

3. To add menu choices to the current menu, click the **Add** button. The Add Choice dialog box appears (see Figure 12.4).

4. Type a menu choice into the **Choice** box, and then click **OK**. You are returned to the Drop-Down Box Properties dialog box, and your menu choice is listed. Add more menu choices as needed.

5. When you have completed adding menu choices, click the **OK** button to close the Drop-Down Box Properties dialog box.

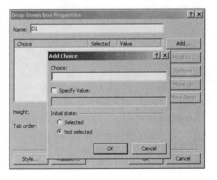

FIGURE 12.4
Use the Add Choice dialog box to add menu choices for your drop-down box field.

TESTING YOUR FORMS

After you create your form, you can quickly test the fields in Preview mode. First, save the page by clicking the **Save** button on the toolbar.

Then click the **Preview** tab at the bottom of the Page window. Your Web page and its form appear as they do on the World Wide Web.

You can fill in text boxes, make check box selections, and test drop-down menus. When you have finished taking a look at your form and its fields, click the **Normal** tab to return to the Page edit mode.

PLAIN ENGLISH

> **Click the Submit Button and Get an Error**   When you cre-ate a form on a page and then publish that page and the rest of the web to a Web server, FrontPage creates a submission page for the form. When you are in Preview mode, this page does not exist (because the web hasn't been published) and so you get an error.

You cannot fully test your form's capabilities until you publish the Web site to a Web server that contains the FrontPage Server Exten-sions. The form feature, like the theme (discussed in the previous lesson) and special component features, does not work correctly unless the Web server contains the appropriate server extensions.

DETERMINING WHERE THE DATA GOES

Because the purpose of creating a Web form is to gather data, you probably want to select the format in which all the collected informa-tion is placed. FrontPage offers different file formats for the submitted data. You can have the data placed in a text file, you can have the data e-mailed to a particular e-mail address, or you can have the data placed directly into a Microsoft Access database.

To select the format for the data collection, follow these steps:

1. Right-click the form and select **Form Properties**. The Form Properties dialog box appears (see Figure 12.5).

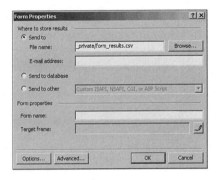

FIGURE 12.5
The Form Properties dialog box enables you to select how the results of your form are saved.

2. Three different possibilities are available for how the data gathered by the form is handled:

   - **Text File**: The default location for the results to be stored is a text file. The text file is stored on the Web server where you publish your web (the _private folder). You need access to the Web server so that you can open the text file and view the contents. Designate a name for that file in the **File Name** box.

   - **E-mail Address**: An alternative to a text file is to have the form results sent to a particular e-mail address. This is useful if you do not have easy access to the Web server where you publish your web. Type an e-mail address in the **E-mail Address** box and then click the **Options** button. Click the **E-mail Results** tab on the Options for Saving Results of a Form dialog box. Enter the **Subject** line that you want placed on the e-mail message that provides the results. Click **OK** to close the dialog box and return to the Form Properties dialog box.

   - **Access Database**: If you want to have your data collected in an Access database (which you would then open in Microsoft Access), click the **Send to Database** radio button and then click **Options**. The Options for Saving Results to Database dialog box opens. Click the **Create** button and a new database is created to contain the data. A message box opens and provides the location of the new database (a folder in the current web) and a data connection phrase such as **Interest**. Write down this information, and then click **OK**. Click **OK** again to close the Options for Saving Results to Database dialog box.

3. After making one of the preceding selections, click the **OK** button to close the Form Properties dialog box.

After you publish your web to a Web server and the form is used by visitors to your site, you can view the data in the text file contained in the _private folder (this folder is automatically created when you create your Web site), or you will receive the data in an e-mail, depending on the choice you made in the Form Properties dialog box.

If you choose to have the results saved in a database, you can directly access the database file using Access. In Access, you have to create a new FTP location in the Open dialog box by clicking the **Look In** drop-down arrow and selecting **Add/Modify FTP Locations**. In the Add/Modify FTP Locations dialog box, enter the FTP address for your Web server (usually **FTP.*servername*.com**) and your username and password. After the FTP location has been created, you can use it to open the database.

An alternative to working in Access is to have the database results displayed on a Web page. The Web page should be held in the _private folder that is part of your web (and is published to the Web server with the other folders and files in the web) because only you have access to the files in the _private folder.

To create a database results page, follow these steps:

1. Go to the Folders view and open the _private folder. Then click the **New Page** button on the Standard toolbar. A new page is placed in the folder.

2. Type in a new name for the page, such as **results.htm** or something similar.

3. Double-click the page to open it in Page view. Place the insertion point where you want to place the database results box.

4. Select the **Insert** menu, point at **Database**, and then select **Results**. The Database Results Wizard appears (see Figure 12.6).

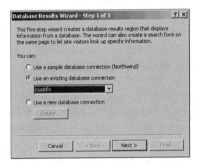

FIGURE 12.6
Using the Database Results Wizard, you can create a results page that allows you to view the data input by visitors to your site.

5. Use the drop-down box to select the database connection for the database that was created when you chose Access database as the collection mode for the data (back in step 3 of the previous set of steps). If you have only created one database connection for the web, it already appears in the drop-down box.

6. Click **Next** to continue. You are asked to select a record source from the database. (This is the table in which the data is placed.) The default table for the new database appears in the Record Source box automatically.

7. Click **Next** to continue. The fields in the database table are displayed. (These are the fields found in the original form that you created.) If you do not want to have all the field information recorded, click **Edit List**. Use the Displayed Field dialog box to remove any fields you don't want. Then click **OK**. When you are ready to move to the next wizard screen, click **Next**.

8. The next wizard screen provides you with the option of displaying the data in one record per row or placing each record in a list. Use the drop-down box to make your selection (see Figure 12.7), and then click **Next**.

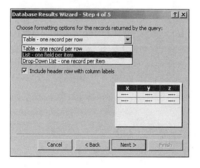

FIGURE 12.7
You can specify how the records in the results list are displayed.

9. The final wizard screen appears; you have the option of displaying all the records together or dividing the records into groups where you specify the number of records in a group. Choose the appropriate option button (and set the number of records in a group, if you use the group option). Click **Finish** to create the results page.

The fields on the original form appear on the database results page. The page only displays results from the form when viewed using your Web browser. And, of course, the web must also be published to the Web server and the Web server must have the FrontPage Server Extensions on it. After the web is up and running and you get some input from visitors, you can then access the results page using your Web browser and view the data.

 TIP

> **File Renamed as ASP File**   When creating forms that supply information to a database or a results page that allows you to view the data collected by the form, you might be prompted to save the Web page with the .asp extension. The extension .asp actually stands for Active Server Pages and is a file format devised by Microsoft to allow Web page interactivity. If prompted to save a page with the .asp extension, do so!

In this lesson, you learned how to create input forms on your Web pages. In the next lesson, you learn to work with FrontPage tables.

LESSON 13
Working with Tables

In this lesson, you learn how to add tables to your Web pages.

USING TABLES ON WEB PAGES

Organizing information on your Web pages so that it's easy to read is a real necessity. One way to group information on a Web page is to use a table. If you have ever worked in a ledger book or used Excel to create a worksheet, you are familiar with the overall look and feel of a table.

Tables provide an excellent way to group numerical information in columns and rows (even displaying a total that summarizes a row or column of information), or tables can be used as layout grids to help you align elements, such as text or graphics, on pages. So although you might typically think of tables as containing numerical data only, you can actually use tables as a nice design feature on your Web pages.

For example, you can create several buttons that act as hyperlinks to other pages or sites (hyperlinks are discussed in Lesson 9, "Working with Hyperlinks"). Or, you can place the button graphics in a table column and add descriptive text for each button in another column of the table, making it easy to align the appropriate graphic with the descriptive text.

To insert a table onto the current Web page, follow these steps:

1. Open the page that will contain the table (double-click the page in Navigation view).

2. Place the insertion point where you want to insert the table.

TIP

> **Quickly Insert a Table Using the Insert Table Button**   You can also place a table onto a page using the Insert Table button on the Standard toolbar. Click the **Insert Table** button, and then drag the mouse to select the number of columns and rows that will be contained in the table. When you release the mouse, the table will be placed on the page.

3. Click the **Table** menu, point at **Insert**, and then select **Table**. The Insert Table dialog box appears (see Figure 13.1).

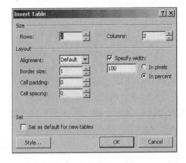

FIGURE 13.1
The Insert Table dialog box enables you to set the parameters for your new table.

4. Use the Rows and Columns spinner boxes to set the number of rows and columns, respectively. To set the alignment for the table, click the **Alignment** drop-down box and select **Left**, **Right**, or **Center** (the Default setting uses the insertion point as the reference point for the table insertion). Spinner boxes are also available for setting the width of the table border, cell padding, and cell spacing (in pixels).

5. When you have completed setting the parameters for the table, click **OK**. The table is inserted at the insertion point (see Figure 13.2).

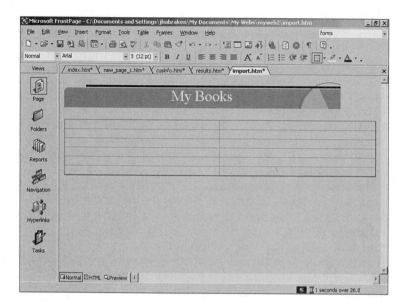

FIGURE 13.2
The new table can be used for numerical information or to align text and graphics on a Web page.

PLAIN ENGLISH

What Is Cell Padding? Cell padding is the distance between the inside border of a cell and the contents of the cell. Cell padding can only be set for all the cells in the table. There is no way to set individual padding settings.

After the table is placed on a page, you can enter text or images into the cells of the table (a *cell* is the intersection of a row and column). Click the mouse pointer in a cell to place the insertion point within it. Then type your text or use the Insert menu to insert some other item. Figure 13.3 shows a table that contains images and text and is used to easily line up a particular text entry with a corresponding image.

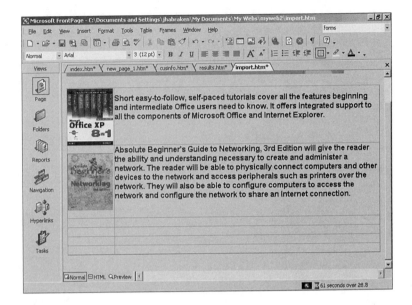

FIGURE 13.3
Tables can contain pictures and text.

INSERTING AND DELETING ROWS AND COLUMNS

Inserting and deleting rows and columns is straightforward. To insert a row or column in the table, follow these steps:

1. Select the row or column that you want to insert a new row or column adjacent to.

2. Select **Table**, point at **Insert**, and select **Rows or Columns**. The Insert Rows or Columns dialog box appears (see Figure 13.4).

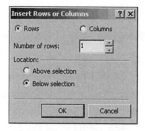

FIGURE 13.4
The Insert Rows or Columns dialog box enables you to insert one or more new rows or columns.

3. Click either the **Rows** or **Columns** option button to select the item you want to insert.

4. Click the up or down arrow or enter a number in the **Number Of** click box to indicate the number of rows or columns you want to insert.

5. In the **Location** area of the dialog box, choose either the **Above Selection** or **Below Selection** option button when you are inserting rows and either the **Left of Selection** or **Right of Selection** option button when inserting columns.

6. When you have made your various selections, click **OK** to insert the new rows or columns.

You can also easily delete columns or rows from your table. Select the rows or columns. Then select the **Table** menu. Click **Delete Cells,** and the selected columns or rows are removed from the table.

CHANGING THE WAY THE TABLE LOOKS

You also have control over the way the table looks, such as the color and width of the table's borders and background and the alignment of the table on the page. Formatting and alignment of a table are controlled in the Table Properties dialog box. However, the look of the table (border and background color) might also be affected by the theme that is currently selected for the page on which the table resides. The theme supplies the default background and border color for the table.

You can change the background color and border width for a table that has been assigned a theme; however, the border color cannot be changed and remains the theme default. The only way to override the theme color is to remove the theme from the page (for more about themes, see Lesson 11, "Using FrontPage Themes").

Follow these steps to change the table background color, border width and color, or the alignment of the table:

1. Right-click the table and select **Table Properties** from the shortcut menu. The Table Properties dialog box appears (see Figure 13.5).

2. To change the color for the table borders, click the **Color** drop-down box in the **Borders** area of the dialog box. Select a new color for the table border.

3. To change the background color of the table, click the **Color** drop-down box in the **Background** area of the dialog box.

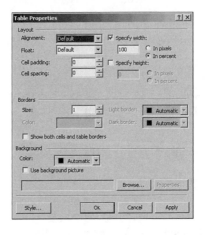

FIGURE 13.5
The Table Properties dialog box enables you to change a number of parameters related to the look of the table.

4. If you want to change the thickness of the table border, use the **Size** click box in the **Borders** area of the dialog box.

5. To change the alignment of the table (Left, Right, Center, or Justify), click the **Alignment** drop-down box and select the appropriate alignment. (This aligns the table on the page, not the text or items within the table cells.)

6. When you have completed setting the various parameters for the table, click the **OK** button to close the Table Properties dialog box and return to the table.

If you want a table with no visible borders, create a new table and then place your text and other items in the table. After you have completely finished placing items in the table, right-click the table and select **Table Properties** from the shortcut menu. Then use the **Borders Size** click box to make the border size **0** (zero) and click **OK**. The items in the table are still aligned (almost magically), but the table borders disappear.

TIP

Using the Mouse to Change Column Widths and Row Heights You can change the column widths and row heights in a table using the mouse. Place the mouse pointer on a column or row border and a sizing tool appears. Click and drag to adjust the column width or row height.

In this lesson, you learned how to create tables on your Web pages and adjust the table settings. In the next lesson, you learn how to add numbered and bulleted lists to your Web pages.

LESSON 14

Creating Bulleted and Numbered Lists

In this lesson, you learn how to add bulleted and numbered lists to your Web pages.

WORKING WITH LISTS

Emphasizing certain information on a Web page is an important aspect of designing Web pages that are easy to read by visitors to your Web site. You can add emphasis to a list of points or delineate a list of items on a Web page by adding numbers or bullets to the items in the list. Numbered lists are great for steps or points that should be read in order. Bulleted lists work best when you want to separate and highlight different items or points in a list, but the items do not have to appear in any particular order.

The style and look of the numbers or bullets that you apply to a list can easily be edited, and you can even change the starting number for a numbered list. The list then renumbers itself automatically. Also, as you add new lines to numbered or bulleted lists, the items are automatically set up with the same numbering style (with the proper number in the list sequence) or bullet style.

ADDING BULLETS TO LISTS

Bullets are great when you want to visually break out a text list from other text on the page. For example, you could list your favorite Web sites in a bulleted list. Bullets also help to make the page more interesting by adding design elements to your Web.

To add bullets to a text list, follow these steps:

1. Use the mouse to place the insertion point where you want to begin your bulleted list.

2. Click the **Bullets** button on the Formatting toolbar. A bullet is placed at the insertion point.

3. Type the text for the first bulleted item in the list.

4. Press **Enter** when you are ready to type the next item. A bullet is placed at the beginning of the line. Type your text.

5. When you have completed your list, press Enter, and then click the **Bullets** button to turn off the bullets.

You aren't limited to bulleted lists that contain only text lines. You can create bulleted lists of hyperlinks. Turn on the Bullets feature (click the **Bullets** button) and then use the Insert menu to insert your list of hyperlinks (see Lesson 9, "Working with Hyperlinks," for more information). Each hyperlink is offset by a bullet as shown in Figure 14.1.

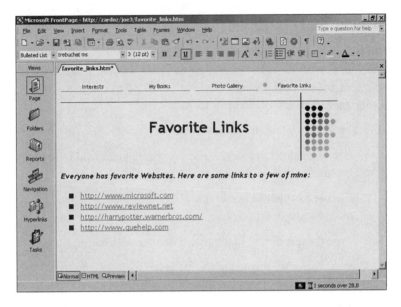

FIGURE 14.1
Bullets can be added to text lists or a list of hyperlinks.

> **TIP**
>
> **Type Your List and Then Add the Bullets**   You can also
> type a list or create a list of hyperlinks and add the bul-
> lets after the fact. Select the list and then click the
> **Bullets** button on the Formatting toolbar.

CHANGING THE BULLET GRAPHIC

The style of the bullets assigned to your list is dictated by the current
theme. If you change the theme, the color, and style of the bullets also
change. You can, however, use any graphic as a bullet, so you do have
the option of replacing the current bullet style with a particular
graphic. The only requirement for the graphic that you use to replace
the bullets is that the image is small (initially created to be the same
relative size as a bullet).

To select a graphic to use as a bullet, follow these steps:

1. Right-click the list to which you assigned the bullets and click **List Properties** on the shortcut menu that appears. The List Properties dialog box appears (see Figure 14.2).

2. In the List Properties dialog box, click the **Specify Picture** option button.

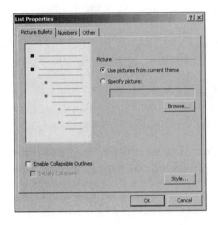

FIGURE 14.2
The List Properties dialog box enables you to select a picture to use as the bullet for the current list.

3. To select the picture to serve as the bullet for the list, click the **Browse** button. The Select Picture dialog box opens.

4. Click the **Select a File on Your Computer** button. The Select File dialog box appears. Use the Select File dialog box to select the picture file and then click **OK**.

5. The name of the picture file appears in the List Properties dialog box. Click **OK** to return to the Web page and assign the new bullet to the list.

The selected graphic replaces all occurrences of the bullet in your list. You can add some nice effects to your Web pages by using special bullets.

WORKING WITH NUMBERED LISTS

Another way to denote the relative importance of the lines in a text list or to put a sequential list together (such as a list of steps) is to add numbering to your text. FrontPage gives you control over the style of the numbers in the list and also gives you the ability to change the start number for the list.

To add numbers to a text list, follow these steps:

1. Place the insertion point where you want to begin your list.

2. Click the **Numbering** button on the Formatting toolbar.

3. Type the text for the first numbered item in the list.

4. Press **Enter** to advance the insertion point down a line. The next sequential number is placed at the beginning of the line.

5. Continue to type text lines as needed. Each time you press **Enter** a new number will be inserted at the beginning of the line.

6. When you have completed your numbered list, press Enter, and then click the **Numbering** button to turn off the Numbering feature. Figure 14.3 shows a numbered list on a Web page.

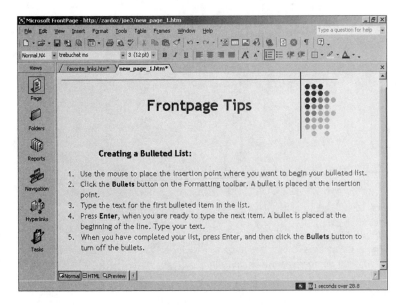

FIGURE 14.3
Numbered lists provide sequential information on your Web page.

CHANGING THE NUMBERED LIST'S ATTRIBUTES

The font and color of the numbers placed on the list depend on the theme that is currently assigned to the page on which you are working. You can change the number style (from Arabic to Roman or to letters of the alphabet), and you can change the start number for the list (to some number other than 1).

Right-click the numbered list and select **List Properties** from the short-cut menu. The List Properties dialog box appears (see Figure 14.4) with the Numbers tab selected. To change the style of the number, select any of the styles provided (such as Roman, letters of the alphabet, and so on) by clicking one of the style boxes. If you want to change the start number, select a new start number using the **Start At** click box.

FIGURE 14.4
The List Properties dialog box provides a Numbers tab that can be used to select a different numbering style or start number.

When you have finished changing the numbered list's properties, click **OK** to close the dialog box. Changes that you make to the style or start number in the list take effect immediately.

 As with bulleted lists, you can also add the numbers to a list after the fact. Select the text or other items in the list (such as hyperlinks) and then click the **Numbering** button on the toolbar. The numbers are added to the list.

In this lesson, you learned how to assign bullets and numbers to lists. You also learned how to change the bullet graphic and the numbering style. In the next lesson, you learn how to use frames on your Web pages.

Lessons 15
Using Frames on Web Pages

In this lesson, you learn how to create a frames page and add inline frames to a Web page.

What Are Frames?

When you build a Web site, it is very important that you create an environment that makes it easy for visitors to navigate the various pages that you place on the site. One way to provide navigation tools for your visitors is to use the Link bars that FrontPage provides (we discussed Link bars and other FrontPage components in Lesson 8, "Inserting Special FrontPage Components").

Another way to setup a navigation system for your visitors is to use frames. A *frame* is a portion or pane of the current Web page that actually displays the content of another Web page. Multiple frames on a single Web page is referred to as a *frameset*. A page containing a frameset is actually allowing multiple pages to be viewed in the browser window at the same time.

For example, one frame or pane in the frameset will show the content of a Web page that has been selected from a list of links that is shown in another frame. The frames containing the navigational links always appear in the browser window, making navigation of the Web site easy. Each frame will also have its own scrollbars making it easy to view the information in each individual frame.

PLAIN ENGLISH

> **frame**   One region of a Web page that is actually made up of a frameset. The content in the frame is actually a separate page designed in FrontPage to be part of the frameset.

PLAIN ENGLISH

> **frameset**   A Web page that is actually a composite of different pages contained in frames. Each frame in the frameset is actually linked to a different page.

Creating a Web page that contains a frameset is a little more complicated than some of the other features that we have looked at in this book. However, FrontPage does provide a number of templates that you can use to create a page containing multiple frames.

CREATING A FRAMES PAGE

Frame pages can be used as the initial home page for a new Web site (providing an easy way to navigate the entire site) or can be added to an existing Web site so that visitors can navigate a particular set of pages in the site. To create a new frames page, follow these steps:

1. In either the Page or Navigation view, select the **File** menu, point at **New** and then select **Page or Web**. The New Page or Web task pane will open.

2. Select the **Page Templates** link in the task pane. The Page Templates dialog box will open. Click the **Frame Pages** tab on the dialog box (see Figure 15.1).

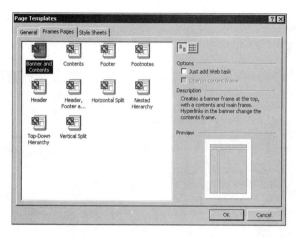

FIGURE 15.1
The Frame Pages tab provides a list of FrontPage frames page templates.

3. A number of different frame pages templates are available on the Frames Pages tab. Click on a particular frame page type to view the number of frames that the template provides.

4. When you locate the frames page you wish to use, select the template icon and then click **OK**. The new frames page will appear in the FrontPage window. The blank frames page will contain a set of buttons in each frame that is used to link a particular web page to the frame (see Figure 15.2).

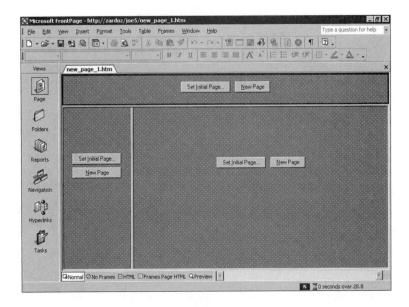

FIGURE 15.2
Buttons are provided in each frame to create the link between the frame and a new or existing Web page.

5. You must link the frame to a new or existing Web page: To link a frame to a new blank Web page, click the **New** page button in the frame. A new blank Web page will appear within the frame.

   To link an existing page to the frame, click the **Set Initial Page** button. The Insert Hyperlink dialog box will appear (see Figure 15.3).

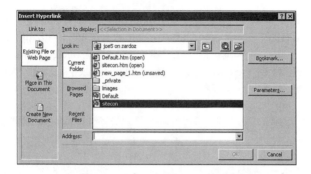

FIGURE 15.3
Select the page that will be linked to the frame.

6. (optional, depending on step 4) Select the page that you wish to link to the frame in the Insert Hyperlink dialog box.

7. (optional, depending on step 4) Click **OK** to close the dialog box.

The current content of the page that is linked to the frame will appear in the frame. If you chose to use a new blank page, the frame will be empty. If you linked an existing page to the frame, the content of that page will appear in the frame.

WORKING WITH FRAME PAGES

Once you have your different Web pages linked to the frames on the frames page, you can place text, graphics, and hyperlinks on these pages (working on them as you would any other page in FrontPage). For example, one page may contain a set of hyperlinks that are used to navigate the site. The links would then appear in the associated frame on the frames page. Another frame may contain nothing more than a banner that will always appear in the associated frame. The main frame on the page would be used to view the different pages that are called up when a link on the links frame is selected.

Figure 15.4 shows a preview of a Frames page that contains three frames. The top frame is linked to a page that contains a banner (just a banner; it always shows at the top of the Frames page). The middle frame will show the current Web page that has been selected from the hyperlinks that are listed on the left frame.

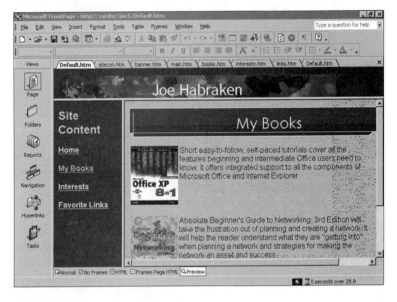

FIGURE 15.4
A frames page containing three frames.

Notice that the currently selected link in the left navigation frame is My Books. The content displayed in the center frame is the content found on a My Books page. The My Books page is shown in Figure 15.5.

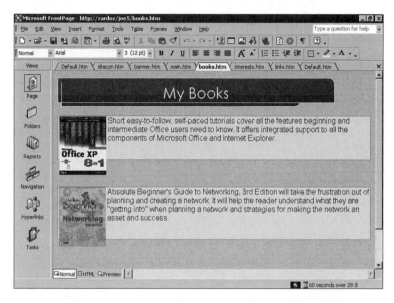

FIGURE 15.5
The Books page that is linked to the My Books Hyperlink.

The great thing about using frames is that each frame is "connected" to a separate Web page, meaning each page can use a different FrontPage theme (discussed in Lesson 11, "Using FrontPage Themes"). This allows you to add more color and graphics to your Web site. Using the frames scheme shown in Figure 15.4, a site could be created where a visitor never leaves the initial page that they open when they first access the Web site.

TIP

Adjust the Size of a Frame   Once you setup the various pages that will appear in the frames on the frame page, you may find during a preview that you need to adjust the size of a particular frame to better show the content. On the frames page, place your mouse on any frame border and use the sizing handle that appears to adjust the size of a particular frame.

ADDING INLINE FRAMES TO WEB PAGES

Another way to take advantage of frames on your Web site without having to create a complex frames page (complex in terms of the fact that each frame has to be linked to a separate Web page) that we have discussed thus far is to use an inline frame. An *inline frame* is a frame (linked to a specific Web page) that can be placed as a pane anywhere on the current page.

Since inline frames can be placed anywhere on the page, they are a little more flexible than the frames you find on a frames page. And you can move an inline frame around on the page as you would any other object.

To add an inline frame to a Web page, follow these steps:

1. If necessary, use the Navigation view to open the page you want to place the inline frame on.

2. Place the insertion point where you wish to place the inline frame.

3. Select the **Insert** menu, then select **Inline Frame**. The inline frame appears on your Web page (see Figure 15.6).

4. You must link the inline frame to a new or existing Web page: to link a frame to a new blank Web page, click the **New** page button in the frame. A new blank Web page will appear within the frame.

   To link an existing page to the frame, click the **Set Initial Page** button. The Insert Hyperlink dialog box will appear.

5. (optional, depending on Step 4) Select the page that you wish to link to the frame in the Insert Hyperlink dialog box.

6. (optional, depending on Step 4) Click **OK** to close the dialog box.

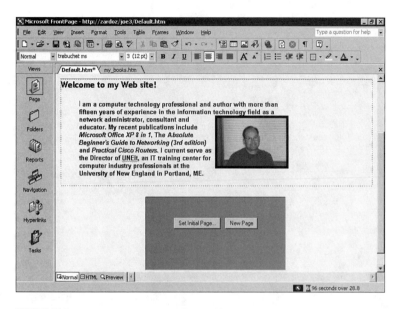

FIGURE 15.6
The inline frame appears on the Web page.

The content inside the inline frame will either be nonexistent (if you are using a new page) or contain the content on the page that you linked to the frame). In the case of a new page, you will have to move to that page in FrontPage and add the appropriate content to the page.

You can adjust the size of the inline frame as needed. Click on the edge of the inline frame so that sizing handles appear around the frame. Then drag the sizing handles to size the frame. Figure 15.7 shows an inline frame on a Web page.

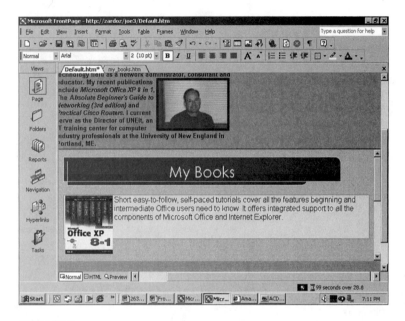

FIGURE 15.7
Inline frames can be used to nest Web pages within other Web pages.

Inline frames will have their own scroll bars. This allows a visitor to manipulate the frame content separately from the content on the page that contains the frame.

In this lesson, you learned how to create a frames page and insert an inline frame on a page. In the next lesson you learn how to add DHTML effects to your Web pages.

Lesson 16
Using DHTML Effects

In this lesson, you learn how to add transitions and other special effects to your Web pages using DHTML.

Understanding DHTML

We have already discussed a number of possibilities for adding interest to your Web pages, such as images, sounds, videos, and FrontPage components. Another way to make your Web pages more exciting is the use of Dynamic HTML (*DHTML*) effects.

DHTML is a Microsoft enhancement to HTML that allows you to animate text and other objects on your Web pages and add page transitions such as vertical blinds and wipes (we will discuss the various page transition types in a moment). DHTML can be used to emphasize information on a page (using a particular effect) or just to make your pages seem a little more "high-tech."

> **PLAIN ENGLISH**
>
> **DHTML**   Dynamic HTML, or DHTML, is a Microsoft HTML enhancement that allows you to animate Web page items and add page transition effects to your FrontPage Web.

Not only can DHTML be used to add special effects to your Web pages, but it can also provide a way to make information on a Web page more accessible and easy to read. For example, you can use DHTML to create collapsible outlines and lists on your Web pages. Let's take a look at page transitions and then we can take a look at animating text and images on your Web pages and creating DHTML outlines and lists.

CAUTION

Know Your Audience   While DHTML could certainly add excitement to your FrontPage Web, it will be no use to the viewers of your Web page if they are not using a Web browser that supports DHTML. Site visitors using older Web pages (such as Internet Explorer 3.0 or Netscape Navigator 3.0) will not be able to view your DHTML effects. If you are creating your Web for an intranet (a Web inside a company) and you know that visitors will be using older versions of the various Web browsers, you may want to forgo the time and effort of adding DHTML effects to your site.

Adding Page Transitions

A page transition is a visual effect that will act on the entire Web page when the page is entered or exited (transitions can also be setup that are triggered when a visitor enters or exits your Web site. The transition is a visual intermediary event as you move to or from the page that you have assigned the transition to. FrontPage offers a number of different page transition types:

- **Wipes**: The contents of the page are cleared from one side of the page to another. For example, a wipe down wipes the page from top to bottom. Up, down, right, and left wipes are available.

- **Blinds**: As the name implies, a blind transition looks like the opening or closing of a window blind. Both vertical and horizontal blinds are available.

- **Box**: The browser window is closed down or opened up using a rectangular frame. Both a box in and box out are available. Figure 16.1 shows a box in transition from one Web page to another.

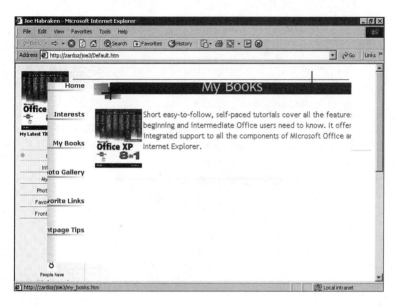

FIGURE 16.1
Page transitions can add interest to your Web site.

- **Circle**: The browser window is closed down or opened up using a circular frame. You can choose from circle in or circle out transitions.

- **Split**: The browser window is split by a vertical or horizontal line that wipes the page either in or out. Vertical and horizontal splits are available.

- **Dissolve**: The Web page is basically pixilated as the text and images on it appear when you access the page.

Other transitions are also available, including the checkerboard (a checkerboard pattern wipes across the screen), random bars (small bars are used as the page is wiped), and strips (which is really just a diagonal wipe). To assign a transition to a Web page, follow these steps:

1. If necessary, use the Navigation view to open the page you want to assign the page transition to (double-click on the page in the Navigation view).

2. Select the **Format** menu, then select **Page Transition**. The Page Transition dialog box will appear (see Figure 16.2).

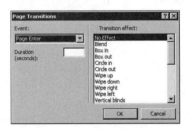

FIGURE 16.2
You can choose from a wide selection of transition effects.

3. Scroll through the **Transition effect** list and select the transition you wish to use.

4. Click the **Event** scroll down list and select how you want the transition event to be triggered: either **Page Enter**, **Page Exit**, **Site Enter**, or **Site Exit**.

5. Click in the **Duration** box and type in the number of seconds you wish the transition to last.

6. Click **OK** to assign the transition to the page.

Make sure that you save the page. You can test the transition by viewing the page in a Web browser. Select the **File** menu and then select **Preview in Browser**. Select the Web browser you will use for the preview in the Preview in Browser dialog box and then click **Preview**. Depending on how you setup the transition (Page Enter versus Page Exit) you may have to navigate to or from the page that you assigned

the transition to actually view it. When you have finished previewing
the transition, you can close the browser window to return to
FrontPage.

TIP

Remove a Page Transition   To remove a page transition,
open the Page Transitions dialog box (select **Format**, then
Page Transition) and select **No Effect** in the Transition
list.

ADDING DHTML EFFECTS TO TEXT AND IMAGES

You can also use DHTML to animate text and images on your Web
pages. For example, you can make text fly onto the Web page or have
a graphic bounce into view. To add DHTML to text and images on a
page, you use the DHTML toolbar.

To add a DHTML effect to text or an image, follow these steps:

1. If necessary, use the Navigation view to open the page you
    want to assign the page transition to (double-click on the
    page in the Navigation view).

2. Select the text or the image that you will assign the DHTML
    effect to.

3. Select the **Format** menu, then select **Dynamic HTML
    Effects**. The DHTML Effect toolbar appears (see Figure 16.3).

4. Click the **On** drop-down box on the DHTML Effect toolbar
    and select the event that will trigger the effect (such as Click,
    Double-click, Mouse over, or Page load; Page load is the
    selection to use when you want effects to happen automati-
    cally).

5. Click the **Apply** drop-down box to select the actual effect,
    such as Fly in, Hop, or Wipe.

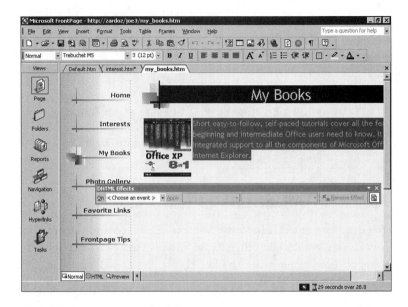

FIGURE 16.3
The DHTML Effect toolbar is used to add effects to selected text and images.

   6. Click the **Choose Settings** drop-down box to select how the
   effect will operate (see Figure 16.4). For example, if you
   selected **Fly in** as your effect, you can have the selected text
   or image fly onto the page from a number of directions such
   as From bottom, From top, From left, and so on.

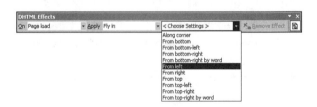

FIGURE 16.4
Use the Choose Settings drop-down list to select how the effect will operate.

7. Press **Ctrl+S** to save the current page and the new effect that you assigned to the selected text or image. You can click the **Close** button on the toolbar if you wish to close it.

Once you have assigned the effect to text or an image, you can preview the effects in a browser window. Select the **File** menu and then select **Preview in Browser**. Select the Web browser you will use for the preview in the Preview in Browser dialog box and then click **Preview**.

If you chose to have the effect event take place when the page is loaded, you can sit back and preview the event. If you selected mouse over or some other mouse manipulation to activate the event, perform that mouse movement. When you have previewed your effect, close the browser window to return to FrontPage.

CREATING COLLAPSIBLE OUTLINES

Another DHTML effect that you can use on your Web pages is the collapsible list. You already learned how to create a numbered list in Lesson 14. And setting up an outline or list so that it collapses on the Web page is just a matter of checking the appropriate checkboxes in the List Properties dialog box when you create your list.

To create a collapsible list and add numbers to a text list, follow these steps:

1. Place the insertion point where you wish to begin your list.

2. Click the **Numbering** button on the Formatting toolbar.

3. Type the text for the first numbered item in the list. Press **Enter** and continue to create the list. If you wish to create different levels in the list, use the **Indent** button on the toolbar to demote items in the list. Press **Enter** twice when you have completed the list.

4. Select the first item in the list (the item at the highest level in the list and then right click. On the shortcut menu that appears, select **List Properties**. The List Properties dialog box will appear (see Figure 16.5).

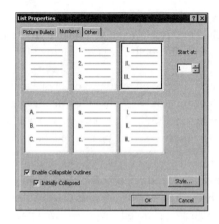

FIGURE 16.5
The List Properties dialog box allows you to enable the DHTML collapsible list.

5. Select the **Numbers** tab of the List Properties dialog box. If you wish to change the number style for the list, select one of the styles shown.

6. Click the **Enable Collapsible Outlines** check box in the dialog box. If you wish the list to start out "collapsed" on the page, click the **Initially Collapsed** check box.

7. Click **OK** to close the dialog box.

You can preview your collapsible list in your Web browser. Select the **File** menu and then select **Preview in Browser**. Select the Web browser you will use for the preview in the Preview in Browser dialog box and then click **Preview**.

Click on the first item in the list to expand the entire list. You can collapse the list by clicking on the first item a second time. Once you have viewed your collapsible list, close the browser window.

In this lesson, you learned how to add DHTML effects to your Web pages. In the next lesson, you learn how to ready your Web for publication by checking hyperlinks and using the Spelling feature.

LESSON 17

Checking Hyperlinks and Spelling

In this lesson, you learn how to verify the hyperlinks in your Web and check the spelling on your Web pages.

BUILDING AN ERROR FREE SITE

Having discussed the basics of using FrontPage to build a Web site, we now need to turn to issues related to getting the Web site ready for publication to the Web. In this lesson we look at verifying the hyperlinks found in your Web and checking the spelling of your text content on your Web pages. In Lesson 18 we will look at using tasks to complete your Web page and then look at how you publish your Web site.

An important aspect of building a visitor-friendly Web site is verifying that all your hyperlinks are operational. FrontPage makes it easy for you to view the hyperlinks on your Web pages. FrontPage can also help you fix broken links by creating a broken hyperlinks report.

Another issue related to creating a good Web site is avoiding typos and misspellings on your Web pages. FrontPage can check the spelling on a single page in your Web or all your Web pages. Let's take a look at how you view and verify hyperlinks and then we will concentrate on the Spelling feature.

VIEWING HYPERLINKS

You can view the hyperlinks for any page in your Web site. Viewing hyperlinks really allows you to get a good idea of how a user will navigate from page to page in the site. The number of hyperlinks that are linked to a particular page will depend on the navigational structure of your site.

For example, you can assume that the home page on a Web would have a fair number of hyperlinks to other pages since it is at the top level in the site's structure. Pages lower in the site's structure would typically have fewer links. However, an exception would be a favorite links page containing a large number of hyperlinks (one for each site you list on the page).

Hyperlinks actually come in two flavors. Hyperlinks that link a page in the Web to another page in the Web is considered an internal link. This is because the target of the hyperlink is part of your site. An external link would be a hyperlink that points to a Web page that is outside your Web site.

To view the hyperlinks for a particular page in the Web, follow these steps:

1. In the Navigation view, select the page that you want to view in the Hyperlinks pane.

2. Click the **Hyperlinks** button on the Views bar. The current page and its hyperlinks will appear in the views pane (see Figure 17.1). The Folder list for your Web also opens in the Hyperlinks view.

3. As shown in Figure 17.1, three pages are linked to the default.htm page (which is the home page for the site and the page that was selected in the Navigation view in Step 1). The hyperlinks for the linked pages shown can also be viewed. Pages with hyperlinks are marked by an Expand button (a plus-symbol) that allows you to expand the hyperlinks for the page; click the **Expand** button to view the hyperlinks for any of the linked pages.

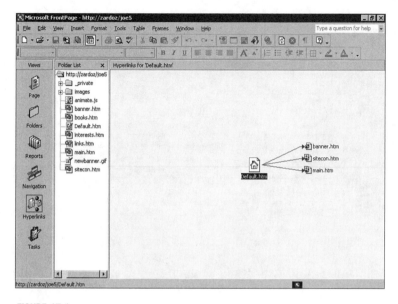

FIGURE 17.1
The Hyperlinks view allows you to view the hyperlinks associated with your Web pages.

4. You can continue to expand the links for subsequent linked pages that appear (click the appropriate **Expand** buttons). This allows you to view much of the hyperlink structure for the site. Figure 17.2 shows the hyperlinks for several pages in a Web.

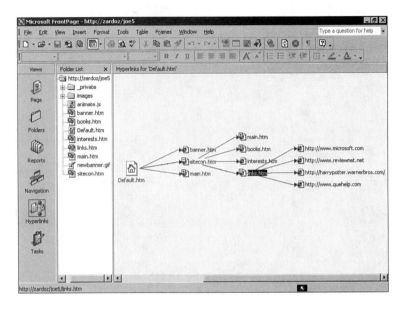

FIGURE 17.2
Expand the Web to view the hyperlink structure of the site.

CAUTION

You Can Only Expand One Path through the Site   When
you expand the hyperlink structure provided in the
Hyperlinks view, you will find that you can only expand
one page at each of the levels in the site. This means
that you can trace a particular hyperlink path through
the site, but you cannot view the entire hyperlink structure for all the pages in the site.

5. To view the hyperlinks associated with another page in the
   Web site, click the page in the Folder list. The Hyperlinks
   view now focuses in on that particular page and its links.

6. When you have completed viewing the hyperlinks, you can
   use the Views bar to move to another view. If you wish to
   view one of the pages shown in the Hyperlinks view in the
   Page view, double-click on that page.

TIP

> **Check Your Picture Hyperlinks**   Because images and
> other graphical elements exist as separate files on your
> Web site, you may want to view what image and other
> media files are hyperlinked to a particular page. In the
> Hyperlinks view, right click on the view pane (the right
> pane) and select **Hyperlinks to Pictures**. This will provide
> a view of all the pictures linked to the current page as
> well as the internal and external hyperlinks.

VERIFYING HYPERLINKS

While viewing hyperlinks in the Hyperlinks view is a good way to get
a good feel for the overall navigational structure of your Web site, you
also need to verify that hyperlinks to images, media files and external
hyperlinks actually work. Visitors to your site will become extremely
disenchanted with your work if you provide a list of Web sites and
these external hyperlinks do not work.

You can actually verify external links in the Hyperlinks view. When
you place the mouse on an external link, a hyperlink tip appears that
says "External Link, the site address and (Not Verified)." Figure 17.3
shows this message as it appears on an external link. This means that
while the hyperlink exists in your Web, FrontPage cannot verify that it
works.

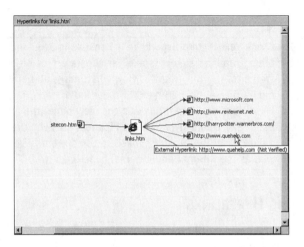

FIGURE 17.3
The status of external links can be checked in the Hyperlinks view.

To verify an external link in the Hyperlink view, right click on any external link and then choose **Verify Hyperlink** from the shortcut menu. You may need to wait for a moment while the site is verified. When you place the mouse on the hyperlink a second time, only the name of the site will appear in the tip; this means the site has been verified.

VIEWING THE BROKEN HYPERLINKS REPORT

Probably a better way to verify the external links in your Web is to use the Broken Hyperlinks report. This allows you to verify all the external links at once and verify hyperlinks to images and other media files.

The Broken Hyperlinks report also makes it easy for you to repair broken hyperlinks. You can double-click on any broken hyperlink in the report and then repair it in the Edit Hyperlink dialog box.

To run the Broken Hyperlinks report, follow these steps:

1. First, save all your Web pages; select **File**, then **Save All**.

2. To run the Broken Hyperlinks report, select the **View** menu, point to **Reports**, point to **Problems**, and then select **Broken Hyperlinks**. The Reports View dialog box appears asking you if you wish to have your hyperlinks verified.

3. Click **Yes** to have the hyperlinks verified.

The Broken Hyperlinks report will appear in the FrontPage window (in the Reports view) as shown in Figure 17.4. The hyperlinks in the Web will be verified (this can take a few minutes if you have a slower Internet connection).

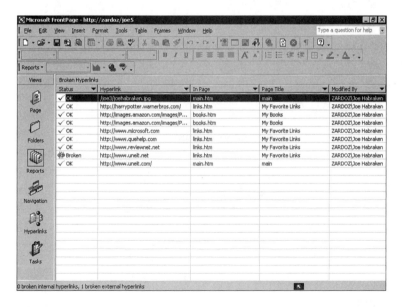

FIGURE 17.4
The Broken Hyperlinks report will verify your links.

Once the hyperlinks have been checked in the Web, each hyperlink in the report will be marked either as "OK," meaning the link works, or as "Broken," meaning the link does not work. Broken hyperlinks will need to be repaired.

TIP

> **You Can Verify Hyperlinks Any Time**   If you did not have your hyperlinks verified when you ran the Broken Hyperlinks report, all the hyperlinks will be marked as "Unknown," meaning they have not been verified. To verify the links, click the **Verify Hyperlinks** button on the Reports toolbar.

REPAIRING A BROKEN HYPERLINK

If you have broken hyperlinks, you can initiate their repair right from the Broken Hyperlinks report. Follow these steps:

1. Double-click on any broken hyperlink that appears in the Broken Hyperlinks report. The Edit Hyperlink dialog box appears (see Figure 17.5).

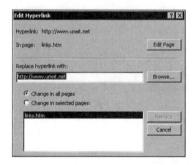

FIGURE 17.5
Use the Edit Hyperlink dialog box to repair broken hyperlinks.

2. If the hyperlink is an external link, you can type the correct address for the hyperlink in the Replace hyperlink with box.

Otherwise, For both internal and external links, click the **Browse** button to open the expand the Edit Hyperlink dialog box.

3. For broken internal links, look in the current folder to locate the Web page that should serve as the internal link. For external links, click the **Browsed Pages** button in the Look in box and locate the URL for the hyperlink.

4. Once you have completed working in the Edit Hyperlink expanded dialog box, click OK. You are returned to the Edit Hyperlink dialog box that was opened in step 1 (and appears in Figure 17.5).

5. Click the **Replace** button. The dialog box will close.

6. Click the Reports icon in the Views bar to return to the Broken Hyperlink report.

When you replace the hyperlink with the new address, you will need to verify that the link works (the hyperlink will be marked "Unknown"). Click the **Verify Hyperlinks** button on the Reports toolbar. The Verify Hyperlinks dialog box will appear. Click the **Start** button in the dialog box. Your edited hyperlinks will be verified.

USING THE SPELLING FEATURE

No matter how flashy your Web site looks or how many great hyperlinks you provide, a Web full of misspelled words and typos will certainly be diminished in the eyes of your site visitors. FrontPage can help you ferret out your misspellings by checking individual pages or the entire Web site.

To check the spelling in the Web, follow these steps:

1. In Page or Navigation view, select the **Tools** menu, and then select **Spelling**. The Spelling dialog box will open.

2. You can check individual pages in the Web for spelling errors, but it probably makes sense to check all the pages; click the **Entire web** option button in the Spelling dialog box and then click the **Start** button.

3. A list of pages with spelling errors (and the misspelling themselves) will be generated in the Spelling dialog box (see Figure 17.6).

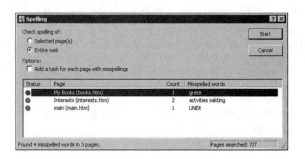

FIGURE 17.6
The Spelling dialog box will provide a list of all the pages in the Web with misspellings.

4. To correct the misspellings on a particular page in the Spelling dialog box list, double-click that page.

5. You will be taken to that page and the Spelling dialog box will offer a list of correct spellings for the first misspelled word on the page (see Figure 17.7).

6. Perform one of the following: Select the correct spelling of the flagged word and click **Change** to correct the word. If the word is correctly spelled and you wish to add it to the dictionary, click the **Add** button. In cases where the word is correct, but you don't wish to add the word to the dictionary, click **Ignore**.

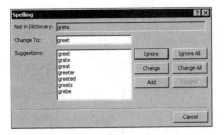

FIGURE 17.7
The Spelling dialog box provides you with suggested spellings.

7. When you have finished checking the current page the Continue with next page dialog box will appear. Click the **Next Page** button to correct the spelling errors on the next page.

8. Repeat steps 5 and 6 as needed to check all the misspellings on your Web pages. When you have completed checking the misspellings on the last page in the Web, the Finished checking pages dialog box will appear.

9. Click the **Back to List** button to return to the Spelling list.

The status of the Web pages appearing in the Spelling dialog box will be changed to Edited. Your Web should now be free from spelling errors. Click the **Close** button on the Spelling dialog box.

In this lesson, you learned how to view and verify the hyperlinks in your Web. You also learned how to use the Broken Hyperlinks report and the FrontPage Speller. In the next lesson you learn how to finish your Web site using tasks and you learn how to publish your Web.

Lesson **18**

Completing and Publishing Your Web Site

In this lesson, you learn how to complete a web using tasks and how to publish your web to the World Wide Web.

Using Tasks to Complete a Web

As you create and fine-tune a web you want to place on the World Wide Web, you will find that you must complete many individual tasks before the site is ready to be published. You have to make sure that graphics or other images have been placed in the appropriate places and that hyperlinks correctly point to their particular destinations. Even the simplest of sites requires you to make changes and improvements to pages in the web, even if you created the web with a wizard.

FrontPage offers a tool for helping you to stay organized as you create and complete a web. FrontPage tasks provide a way to keep a running list of your web duties as you work on the site. This Tasks list can be viewed any time in the Tasks view.

You will find that tasks are automatically created by some of the FrontPage wizards, such as the Corporate Presence Wizard. Figure 18.1 shows a list of tasks associated with a new web created using the Corporate Presence Wizard.

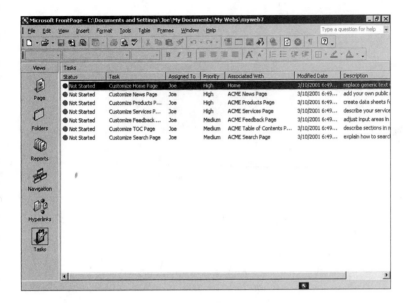

FIGURE 18.1

Tasks are automatically created by some of FrontPage's web wizards.

CREATING A NEW TASK

You can create tasks and link them to an entire web page or to items on that page, such as pictures or other objects. The easiest way to create a new task that is linked to a particular page is to create the task with the page in the Page view. For example, suppose you have a page that will contain hyperlinks to your favorite sites. You can create a task for this page to make sure you've placed all the appropriate hyperlinks (to your favorite sites) on the page before you publish the web.

Follow these steps to create a new task:

1. Open the page (double-click it in the Navigation view) for which you want to create a task.

2. Select the **File** menu, point at **New**, and then select **Task** (or select **Edit**, **Task**, and **Add Task**). The New Task dialog box opens (see Figure 18.2).

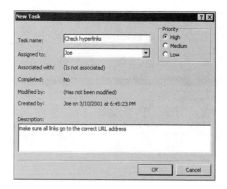

FIGURE 18.2
The New Task dialog box is where you name, set the priority for, and describe your new task.

3. Type a task name into the Task Name box. To assign a priority to the task (other than the default, which is Medium), click the appropriate option button in the Priority area.

4. Type a description for the task into the Description box.

5. Click **OK** to create the new task.

The new task is created and linked to the current page. To view the new task, click the **Tasks** button on the Views bar.

TIP

> **Create Your Task List Up Front**   To help you plan the work flow on a new Web site, create the tasks for that web as soon as you (or a wizard) create the pages for that web. Staying organized ensures that your site is complete before you place it on the World Wide Web.

STARTING A TASK

After you create the task (or several tasks), you can view the task in the Tasks view. This view is also where you start a task, mark a task as complete, or delete an unwanted task.

To start a particular task, follow these steps:

1. In the Tasks view, double-click the task you want to start. The Task Details dialog box opens (see Figure 18.3).

FIGURE 18.3
Start your task using the Task Details dialog box.

2. Click the **Start Task** button.

FrontPage takes you to the page or other object to which the task was linked. For example, if your task is to create hyperlinks on a particular page, you are taken to that page where you can begin creating the needed hyperlinks.

COMPLETING A TASK

After you finish a particular task, you can mark that task as completed. Saving the page that the task was assigned to does this. Follow these steps:

1. Click the **Save** button on the toolbar. A message box appears, letting you know that this page was opened from the Tasks view.

2. To mark the task as completed, click **Yes** (if you haven't completed the task but want to save your changes, click **No**, and you can complete the task at a later time).

When you return to the Tasks view (click the **Tasks** icon on the Views bar), the task is marked as completed. You can also mark tasks as completed directly in the Tasks view. Right-click the task and select **Mark Complete** on the shortcut menu that appears.

If you find that you end up with redundant tasks or create a task that doesn't end up fitting into your web plan—for example, you might want to delete the page associated with the task—you can easily delete any task on the list. Right-click the task and select **Delete** on the shortcut menu. FrontPage asks whether you want to delete the current task. Click **Yes** to delete the task.

CAUTION

> **Check the Web Reports**   Even if you use tasks to make sure that you cover all the details related to your web, check the Reports view before publishing the site. Reports concerning unverified or broken hyperlinks or unlinked graphics (these reports are generated automatically by FrontPage) can help you avoid the embarrassment of publishing a Web site that doesn't work the way you intended it to.

PUBLISHING YOUR WEB

After you have finished your site (check the Tasks view to decide whether you are truly finished), you are ready to publish the web. Publishing the web means that you place all the folders and files in the web onto a Web server. The Web server then serves up your site to visitors on the World Wide Web.

You can take two routes to get your web onto your Web server: You can use HTTP (Hypertext Transfer Protocol) to upload your web to the server, or you can use FTP (File Transfer Protocol) to move the files.

If you use HTTP, the server you send your web files to must have the FrontPage server extensions installed on it. You should check with your Internet service provider before you upload a FrontPage web to the server to be sure the extensions are available.

If the server is not enabled with the FrontPage extensions, you can still upload to your Web server by using FTP. Be advised, however, that Web servers that do not support the FrontPage extensions preclude you from using special components on your Web pages—for example, FrontPage hit counters and themes might not work correctly.

Specifying whether you are publishing your site using HTTP or FTP is determined by how you enter the address for the Web server into the FrontPage Publish Web dialog box (covered in detail in the steps that follow). For example, suppose your Web server on the World Wide Web is called joe.com. If you are using HTTP to upload your web files, this server's address is specified as http://www.joe.com. If you are using FTP to upload the files, the address for this site is ftp.joe.com.

To publish your web, follow these steps:

1. Connect to the Internet using your dial-up connection to your Internet service provider.

2. In FrontPage, select the **File** menu and then select **Publish Web**. The Publish Destination dialog box appears (see Figure 18.4).

FIGURE 18.4
Enter your Web site's address into the Publish Destination dialog box.

3. Enter the address of the server that you will upload your web to in the **Enter Publish Destination** box (using either an HTTP or FTP address, as discussed earlier in this section). Click **OK**.

4. The Publish Web dialog box appears (see Figure 8.5). This box displays all the files in your web. If the web has been published previously to the address you specified in step 3, you can see the files currently stored on the Web server by clicking the **Show** button. This opens a second pane in the Publish Web dialog box showing the destination server and the web files it contains.

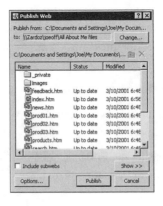

FIGURE 18.5
The Publish Web dialog box is where you select publishing options.

5. (optional) If you are publishing this web to update a Web site that has been published previously, you can choose to update only pages that have changed since the last time you published the web. Click the **Options** button on the Publish Web dialog box. The Options dialog box appears.

6. (optional) In the Options dialog box, click the **Changed Pages Only** option button, and then click **OK** to return to the Publish Web dialog box.

7. If the current web contains hyperlinks to other webs that you have created but not published (called subwebs), select the **Include Subwebs** check box to publish these along with the current web.

8. Click the **Publish** button.

You are kept apprised of the progress of the publishing of your web while you wait. When the process has completed, click the **Done** button to close the notification box.

Your web is now available on the World Wide Web. You can use your Web browser to visit your Web site and be sure it is functioning correctly. If you need to modify pages or update the Web site, modify the original web in FrontPage and then publish the web to the server again, making sure that you check the option for changed pages to replace pages already on the server.

INDEX